Demystifying Sport

A Guide To Pretending You Know What's Going On

Demystifying Sport

A Guide To Pretending You Know What's Going On

By

David Gladstone

Edited by AnnMarie Reynolds

Published by begin a book Independent Publishers

www.beginabook.com

First paperback edition published in the United Kingdom 2024.

ISBN: 978-1-915353-28-3 (paperback)

Book Cover by AnnMarie Reynolds (some content AI generated)

Interior Illustrations by AnnMarie Reynolds

Interior Images/Photographs licensed for Commercial Use from Adobe Stock including some AI generated elements.

Published by begin a book Independent Publishers

begin a book
www.beginabook.com

For the curious minds eager to explore the world of sports. May this book be your first step towards understanding and enjoying the glorious sports contained within.

Contents

Introduction

I do not pretend to be an expert in any sport, rather, I am a casual watcher, but like many, I understand some sports more than others. Which has, over the years, affected my enjoyment. This got me thinking …

… what if there was a book, a coffee table companion if you like, which answered some of those niggling questions like …

- In **Cricket**, why doesn't the batsman just try to whack every ball?
- In **Formula One**, why doesn't everyone drive the same car so the contest is about driver skill?
- In the **Tour de France**, why do some riders take all the brunt of the wind?
- In **Football**, why do players miss penalties?

… and essentially, made us all look like sporting geniuses?

So, on the basis I couldn't find one, I decided (admittedly a long time ago) that I would write one, and now, I am thrilled to present (admittedly after a very long time) the fruits of my labours.

I humbly welcome you to, *Demystifying Sport – A Guide To Pretending You Know What's Going On.*

This, you will discover, is no ordinary sports book. In fact, it couldn't be more different. It is the half-time orange of sports books. The cucumber sandwich of sports books. The strawberries and cream of sports books. The … you get the idea.

It's a sports book within a sports book and covers no less than seven of the most popular sports in the world. Each has an entire section dedicated to basic and more in-depth information which has been designed to give you just enough knowledge for boasting rights, but not so much that you require copious cups of coffee to get through it.

9

When I first started writing and researching, I found the internet packed with information; however, to me, it didn't seem easily digestible. I had to research my research, which was confusing, to say the least, so I have removed the confusion for you by presenting what you need in an easy-to-follow format. There are no lengthy paragraphs of technical information; any sources you might need for further reading are referenced in the footnotes which means you can decide what bits you want to explore in more detail.

My goal (pardon the pun) is for you to enjoy this book – which is why there are also *fun facts* littered throughout each chapter, as well as a *multiple-choice quiz* at the end.

Within each sport, I have tried to cover essential information, such as key personnel and decisions that need to be made. I also aim to provide a solid grounding in the way each sport works, for example, how points are scored, how races are run, and what the main trophies and tournaments are. Useful stuff, things you might hear commentators saying, phrases and quotes you can impress your friends with ... in essence, everything I could think of to make your understanding of the wonderful world of sport a bit more straightforward.

I mentioned including seven sports, which I chose based on extensive research – okay, I asked my friends – but also on my own interests and those which I believe generate the most public interest and sponsorship. That's not to say there aren't other sports which also fall into this premise, but I wanted it to be a book, not a house brick, so the seven I chose to include are:

- Cricket
- Football
- Formula One
- Golf
- Rugby (Union)
- Tennis
- Tour de France

Other nuggets you will find within these pages:

- Technology and its use in sport.
- The duration of each sport, i.e., 80 minutes, two hours, no set time, four days, five days or 21 days.

- Equipment – what is used and needed and its (sometimes eye-watering) cost.
- What you get for winning – and losing.
- The officials and their roles.
- Communication within the sport, between teams, players, managers, etc.
- Weather conditions and how they affect each sport.
- And, of course, the history of each sport.

I hope that what you learn will enable you to join in conversations you felt otherwise excluded from, or maybe you'll discover a new hobby or find yourself winning the sports round in a pub quiz or in Trivial Pursuit (does anyone still play Trivial Pursuit?).

You will also gain an understanding of the attraction of these sports and why it is they have such a faithful fan base and following. In summary, your eyes will be opened to a whole new world of sport in a way that is fun, informative and above all, easily digestible.

Dive in wherever you like—you don't need to read it from cover to cover. You can pick and choose what you want to know. Perhaps you could even host a *Demystifying Sport Party* where you play the quiz and test your new-found knowledge amongst friends.

All of this is now at your fingertips, so without further ado, I would like to thank you for choosing to *Demystify Sport* and encourage you to turn the page and embrace this journey.

And, above all, have fun!

Best wishes,

David.

PS. Just a heads-up: This book is based on current rules which were correct at the time of publication in September 2024. If you are reading after this time, some (or all) of the rules may well be out of date! If your question or understanding of a particular sport and its rules is critical (i.e. you're just about to win that pub quiz!), then I strongly recommend checking the latest facts.

Chapter One

CRICKET

"In cricket, as in life, you need to have a game plan and execute it with determination."

Rahul Dravid

CONTENTS

1. What is Cricket?

Cricket is a game played with a bat and ball between two teams of eleven players on a grass field. In the middle (roughly) of the field, there is a 22-yard pitch with a wicket at each end. The wicket consists of three wooden stumps and two wooden bails, which are balanced on top of the stumps.

Cricket in a nutshell:

A bowler bowls the ball to the batter, who tries to hit it. If they hit the ball far enough, they will run from one end of the pitch to the other (between the wickets) in order to score runs. There is a batter at both 'ends' of the pitch and depending on how many times they run up and down the pitch after a shot, dictates which of the two batters is then 'on strike', i.e. to line up to face the next ball. The team with the most runs after both teams have been bowled out (more later on how a batter is 'out') wins the match.

When a final score is given, it may be declared as either:

- Team A won by 76 runs. This means that Team B would have batted last and was 76 runs short of their opponent's score when they were all out.

  OR

- Team B won by three wickets. This means that Team B achieved its target and only lost seven of its batters in the process. Therefore, they had three batters left to play if they needed them, hence the three wickets.

For those unfamiliar with cricket, it can be a hard game to follow, with many complex rules. With this guide, my aim is to simplify it as best I can.

2. Equipment

- For batting, you need a wooden bat, padded gloves, a box, pads for the legs, and a helmet.
- For bowling – a ball made of cork covered in leather which is rock hard.
- Wicket-keeper – pads and specialist gloves.

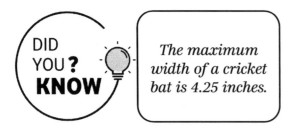

- Umpires - a white coat which has big pockets to hold light meters (to check if it is light enough to play safely) and many other useful objects.
- Two sets of three wooden stumps and four bails (two for each set of stumps).

In 1771, an English player, Thomas White, arrived at the batting crease holding a bat as wide as the three stumps. The bat completely obscured the stumps, which meant it was virtually impossible for the opposition to hit the stumps with the ball to get him out (known as bowled out). The opposition protested, and the laws were changed, but not until 1774.

3. History

It is widely believed that cricket may have been invented by children living in the Weald, an area with dense woodlands and clearings in the southeast of England during the Saxon or Norman times. The first recorded instance of cricket being played as an adult sport dates back to 1611. Some people think that cricket may have evolved from bowls. The similarity being that in bowls, the aim is to place a ball in the way to prevent the opponent's ball from reaching the target (the jack ball), and in cricket, the batter tries to do the same job - block the ball from hitting the stumps.

Village cricket became popular during the middle of the 17th century, and by the second half of the century, the first English county teams were formed. The earliest professionals were experts in village cricket, and it was on the 27th of June 1709, that the first game was played between two county teams. A match took place between teams representing Kent and Surrey at Dartford, and whilst the result was not recorded, it is known that the teams played for a wager of £50.

The first Laws of Cricket were written in 1744 and amended again thirty years later to include innovations such as the lbw rule, a third stump (middle), and a maximum bat width. These laws were created by the 'Star and Garter Club', whose members established the famous Marylebone Cricket Club (MCC) at Lord's in 1787. The MCC became the custodian of the Laws immediately after their formation.

Prior to the formation of the MCC, the Hambledon Club in Hampshire was the centre of the game for about thirty years. Lords Cricket Ground opened in 1787 and was named after Thomas Lord, the founder of the MCC.

Cricket was introduced to North America through English colonies as early as the 17th century, and in the 18th century, it spread to other parts of the world. Colonists brought it to the West Indies, whilst British East India Company Mariners introduced it to India.

Cricket arrived in Australia almost immediately after colonisation began in 1788 and went on to reach New Zealand and South Africa in the early 19th century.

4. Formats of Cricket

There are three main formats of cricket currently played at International level: Test Matches, One-Day Internationals (ODIs), and Twenty20 (T20) Internationals. Another format, The Hundred, is also in existence, though this is a very recent addition.

For the sake of brevity (he said with tongue firmly in cheek), this book will concentrate primarily on Test Match cricket with a brief reference to the other formats as many of the rules and tactics apply to all formats. Whichever your preferred type of cricket, therefore, I hope to provide you with a good, basic grounding.

Test Cricket

Test Cricket is the oldest and most traditional form of the game, having been played since 1877. The format has now settled on five days in duration, with each match consisting of two innings per side. This format is considered the pinnacle of the game because it tests teams over a longer period of time and allows the team captains maximum flexibility when determining tactics. To succeed in this format, players must demonstrate endurance, technique and composure in all kinds of conditions.

One Day Internationals

One Day Internationals are a shorter and faster format. They consist of one innings of 50 overs per team and have a different set of rules to those in place for Test Cricket.

For example, each bowler is limited to bowling only ten overs in one-day matches, whereas in Test Cricket, there are no such limitations. The pinnacle event in this format is the Cricket World Cup, which is contested every four years.

The first One Day International (ODI) cricket match was played on 5 January 1971 between Australia and England at the Melbourne Cricket Ground. The original Test Match had been washed out due to rain, so, after careful consideration, the officials made the decision to cancel the match and organise a new one instead. They proposed a one-off one-day game consisting of 40 overs per side. Australia won the game by 5 wickets (meaning that they batted second and passed England's total with five wickets to spare).

T20 Internationals

T20 Internationals are the shortest and fastest form of the game. Consisting of 20 overs per side, this format has brought new audiences to cricket since its advent in 2005 and has also triggered new skill sets and innovations from players and coaches. A Twenty20 International match is usually completed in three hours and is characterised by powerful batters who can hit the ball a long way, skilful bowling and athletic fielding. Even though it hasn't been around for very long (comparatively), T20 has become hugely popular with fans around the world.

5. Test Cricket – Digging Deeper

The oldest and most prestigious form of cricket is Test cricket. Matches last a maximum of five days, with play taking place from 11:00 a.m. until 6:00 p.m., with breaks for lunch and tea (after all, cricket was invented in England!). The breaks run from 1.00 p.m. to 1.40 p.m. and 3.40 p.m. and 4.00 p.m. Each day of play is divided into three two-hour sessions.

In this form of the game, players wear white clothing and use a red ball. Each team bats all the way through its line-up twice (for a total of four innings), and the team with the most runs in their two innings combined wins the match. An innings typically lasts between one and two full days, and the batting team often scores between 200 and 400 runs in each innings. If the four innings have not been completed at the end of five days, the match is declared a draw. If one team feels that it has scored enough runs in either innings and they still have batters waiting to bat, it can 'declare' its innings closed (known as declaring) early (before each batter has been dismissed) so as to provide enough time to get the opposition out.

AI representation of Test Cricket whites

To some, the idea of a game being drawn after five days is ridiculous. However, many of the most memorable matches have ended up being drawn. For example, in Port of Spain Trinidad in 2009, England set the West Indies a target of 240 runs to win the game. On the final day, the batting team had been reduced to just 90 runs for the loss of six wickets (sometimes depicted as 90 for 6 or 90/6). This meant the West Indies still needed a further 150 to win the match, but with six of their best batters back in the pavilion, it seemed a long shot. Somehow, they managed to hold on, though, ending the fifth and final day on a score of 114 for 8, which was 126 runs short. By managing to stay in until the end of the day, they had denied England victory, and this fabulous rear-guard action saved them from losing the match.

Originally Test matches had no time limit and could last for days and days. The five-day maximum was only introduced after a famous match between England and South Africa in 1939, which had to be abandoned after nine days of play because the England team would have missed their boat back to London.

There is no Test Cricket World Cup. It would be logistically unworkable to stage any sort of meaningful multi-team tournament when each match can last up to five days. Instead, nations take turns playing each other in a series of three or five-matches, either home or away. Traditional rivals of similar strength will often play four or five Test matches in a series every two years, alternating between home and away. The status of 'best in the world' is then determined by Team Rankings based on results. At the moment (May 2024), Australia are at the top of the test rankings, followed by India and England.

6. Where is Cricket Played?

The obvious answer is on a cricket pitch. But where are some of the most famous grounds?

- Lords - London – often referred to as the home of cricket.
- Kensington Oval – Bridgetown, Barbados.
- Eden Gardens – Kolkata, India.

- Melbourne Cricket Ground (MCG) - Melbourne, Australia.
- Newlands – Cape Town, South Africa.
- Galle International Ground – Galle Sri Lanka.

All international cricket grounds have what is known as an 'honours board', which is located in the Pavilion. As the name suggests, it is an 'honour' for a player to have their name on the board, and to achieve this, a player needs to score a hundred runs in one innings (colloquially known as a ton) or take five opposition wickets in one innings.

7. The Cricket Ground

A cricket field, or ground, is a roughly circular field of flat grass ranging in size from about 120 to 200 metres (130 to 220 yards) across. The boundary (edge) is defined by a rope covered with advertising 'toblerones' (triangle-shaped pieces of foam that are lightweight and easily moved). Advertisers pay to have their names displayed on these 'toblerones'.

Often you will see several 'pitches' in the centre of the ground, on either side of the main playing pitch. These are used for warm up and practice. (AI representation)

The field is divided into four parts. When the batter stands 'on strike' in the middle of the pitch, the areas around them are referred to as:

- The side of the field in front of them is the offside.
- The side of the field behind them is the leg side or onside.
- The half of the field in front of the batter's wicket is known as forward of square.
- The half of the field behind the batter's wicket is referred to as behind square or backward of square.

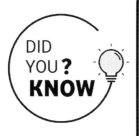
At both ends of the ground, in line with the pitch, are large white screens that deliberately contrast with the colour of the red ball. These are known as 'sight screens' and form a uniform background behind the bowler. The screens are there to make it easier for the batter to see the ball as it is being bowled–crucially when it is leaving the bowler's hand.

8. The Cricket Pitch

In the middle of the (roughly circular) field lies the pitch, which is a carefully prepared rectangle of closely mown and rolled grass. It is marked at either end with white lines known as creases.

The two wickets are placed facing each other, one in the middle of each bowling crease, as shown on the diagram. The popping creases extend parallel to each other and are usually marked for several metres beyond the pitch area.

Note: The popping crease is a guideline for batters because it denotes the 'safe' area in which they must remain to negate the possibility of being 'run out'. If they are outside of this area, batters are considered to be 'out of their ground', and if the stumps are hit with the ball by the opposing team, they will be run out.

Wicket Confusion!

The word 'wicket' is extensively used in Cricket and, in order to add to the confusion, it can be used in three different ways:

- The three stumps are often referred to as **the wicket**.
- The pitch is also referred to as **the wicket**.
- When a fielding team dismisses a batter, they are said to have **'taken their wicket'**.

The Cricket Pitch

A properly prepared pitch is very hard—almost like concrete. The ground workers at each pitch aim to prepare it to be as flat as possible so that the ball bounces evenly. An even and reliable bounce is hugely beneficial to both the batting and fielding sides; however, as a match progresses, the pitch may begin to develop irregularities, including cracking of the surface.

9. Some Laws of the Game

How the game is played

- Each team consists of 11 players, including a specialist wicket-keeper.
- All 11 of the fielding team take to the field, as well as two from the batting team and two umpires.
- The two batters take up their positions at either end. One batter is 'on strike' (facing the bowler to receive the ball), and their partner (standing at the other end of the pitch with the wicket-keeper) is referred to as the non-striker.
- In front of each set of stumps, a chalk line (or crease) is drawn. As long as either the batter or their bat are on or inside the crease, they cannot be run out or stumped.

Cricket Pitch Dimensions
(not to scale)

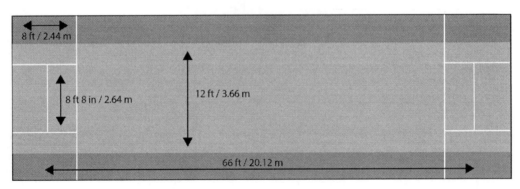

8 ft / 2.44 m

8 ft 8 in / 2.64 m

12 ft / 3.66 m

66 ft / 20.12 m

- A substitute player is allowed if a player is injured, but the substitute can only field. They are not permitted to bat or bowl.

One player from the fielding team bowls the ball to the 'on strike' batter. With their wooden bat, the striker tries to hit the ball around the ground and score 'runs'. Runs are scored in a number of ways:

a. The two batters run between the two sets of stumps, crossing past each other as they do. They continue to run up and down the wicket until the fielding team returns the ball. Each time they run successfully, a score of 'one run' is added to the batters' score.

b. The batter hits the ball over the rope boundary line, with the ball bouncing or hitting the field before crossing the boundary line. This automatically scores the striking batter four runs and they do not need to run (though they may begin running until they are sure the ball has reached the boundary).

c. The batter hits the ball over the boundary line and the ball does not hit the field first. This automatically scores the striking batter six runs and the same comment as scoring a four applies, in respect to running.

There are other, more unusual ways to score runs, such as overthrows and no balls, but for the purposes of this simple guide, these are the three main ways.

The fielding team has two aims:

(1) to get the batters out and
(2) to limit the number of runs they score.

There are three wooden stakes at each end of the pitch, which are known as the stumps. Two wooden pieces, called bails, rest on top of the stumps, giving the look of a small wooden castle. The collective name for the stumps and bails is a wicket. The three stumps are individually named as the 'middle stump (fairly self-explanatory) the 'off stump' and the 'leg stump'. If the batter is right-handed, and you are looking at the stumps from the bowler's end, the one on the left is the leg stump, and the other is the off stump. They reflect the two sides of the pitch.

Before the match starts, the coach and captain will choose their eleven players to form the team. They will need to consider how many specialist batters they want and how many bowlers to include. Some players can both bowl and bat. As they are specialists in neither discipline, they are known as 'all-rounders' who are great assets due to their versatility. The team will also have a specialist wicket-keeper.

When it is time to field, the captain will determine where on the ground their players should be positioned, depending upon:

- The relative skill of the batter
- The strategy developed by the fielding team to get the batter out
- The relative skill and type of bowler – will they be bowling fast or slow?
- The stage of the game

The eleven members of the fielding team will consist of one 'bowler' who delivers the ball to the batter, one 'wicket-keeper' who stands behind the batter to receive the ball if it is not hit by the batter or catch it if it is, and the remaining nine players arrange themselves around the ground to catch or field the ball. The bowler is required to deliver the ball with a straight arm, which means throwing is not permitted, and they also have to use a windmill action to deliver the ball, which must bounce once on the pitch before reaching the batter. There is a delivery known as a 'full toss', which can also be used. In this instance, the ball does not bounce before it reaches the batter.

There are no restrictions on the batting style, but the traditional stance is similar to that of baseball, where the bat is held at hip level with the end pointing back towards the wicket-keeper. The batters wear pads on both legs, a thigh pad, a 'box', gloves and a helmet for protection. Interestingly, boxes have been used to protect male cricketers' sensitive areas since the 16th century, while helmets were not used to protect their heads (arguably of greater importance?) until the 1970s.

Law Enforcement!

The laws of cricket (not rules) are enforced by umpires – two of whom will be out on the field of play. A third umpire (off the field) will make some of the difficult decisions, such as whether a catch has been taken correctly or if a ball has gone over the boundary. The third umpire will often use television replays to help with decision-making.

In front of each set of stumps is drawn a chalk line or 'crease' to mark the area that essentially 'belongs' to the batter. As long as they or the end of their bat remains inside the crease—with the bat still being held by the batter—they are safe from being 'run out'. Note: the crease 'in' area is measured from between the stumps and the crease line.

Cricket Umpire standing at square leg

Before the match starts, there is a coin toss. The captain from the away team calls heads or tails, and then the captain of the team winning the toss gets to choose whether their team will bowl or bat first. There are reasons for choosing both.

<u>Batting First</u>

In Test cricket, it has generally been believed that batting first is the best strategy. This is because it allows the batters to play on a pitch that is expected to be easier to bat on than it will be later in the match. The bowlers, on the other hand, can take advantage of the increasingly challenging pitch on the final day of the match. (Batting first means Team A will bat innings 1 and 3, and Team B will bat innings 2 and 4). The pitch will be considerably worn by the time the game reaches innings 4, which is usually beneficial for the bowlers. This is because there might be holes or cracks in the ground that can positively affect the bounce of the ball).

Other reasons to bat first:

• 'Runs on the board' – the pressure for the team batting second after the first team have scored a big total. Also known as Scoreboard Pressure.

• It gives the captain the chance to take control of the game – the captain can adjust how fast the team scores, when to declare, etc.

• The team fielding first can be worn down, particularly if they have to field for an extended period of time. If the batting team are playing well, all eleven players of the fielding side could well be on the pitch fielding for two days! Which is hard work.

Bowling First

Having said that, the captain may decide to bowl first if they consider the conditions (largely determined by the weather) favourable for bowling. Conditions that favour bowling usually occur when the sun isn't shining, and the sky is overcast. Bowlers can often make the ball move about more than usual when it's like this, which makes life harder for batters.

10. Cricket Simplified?

As already mentioned, cricket can seem confusing to the uninitiated, so the following, which was written in the 1970s, might (or might not!) help:

- You have two sides, one out in the field and one in.

- Each man that's in the side that's in goes out, and when he's out, he comes in, and the next man goes in until he's out.

- When they are all out, the side that's out comes in, and the side that's been in goes out and tries to get those coming in, out.

A batter cannot be given out unless the fielding team appeals, even if the criteria for dismissal are met!

- Sometimes, you get men still in and not out.

- When a man goes out to go in, the men who are out are trying to get him out, and when he is out, he goes in, and the next man in goes out and goes in.

- There are two men called umpires who stay out all the time, and they decide when the men who are in are out.

- When both sides have been in, and all the men have been out, and both sides have been out twice after all the men have been in, including the not outs, that's the end of the game!

11. Playing Cricket

The bowler runs up to one end of the pitch and bowls the ball to the 'on strike' batter who is standing at the other end of the pitch, guarding their stumps. The batter attempts to hit the ball to a vacant area, in order to score runs. Depending on the quality of the ball bowled and their objective, they will decide whether to attack or defend or, indeed, whether to let the ball go by.

As mentioned earlier, batters play in pairs. If Batter A hits the ball to a vacant part of the field, the two batters may (but are not obliged to) run from their end of the pitch to the other, passing each other as they go. If both successfully make it from one end to the other without the fielding team striking their stumps with the ball, one run is added to the batter and the team's score. Now, Batter B is on strike, and the next ball will be bowled to them while Batter A stands at the non-striker's end. This continues for six deliveries (which are collectively known as an 'over'). Then, the bowler has a rest, and the following over is bowled from the other end by their bowling partner.

The rule that one run is scored for running once technically extends to infinity. If Batters A and B manage to run all the way up and all the way back, their team scores two runs and so on. In practice, there is a limit to how many times the batters can physically run the 22 yards between each end before the fielding team retrieves the ball, so it is uncommon to see batters score more than three runs in one go.

As previously mentioned, the batter can also score runs by hitting the ball all the way to the boundary at the perimeter of the ground. If the ball is hit to the boundary, touching the ground at least once, the batting team scores four runs. If the ball is hit all the way over the boundary, the batter scores six runs. These are simply known as 'fours' and' sixes'. The batters do not need to run in these situations.

Sometimes, a delivery may produce no action. The batters may choose not to play at the ball and let it sail harmlessly to the wicket-keeper or may choose to hit the ball with their bat but then not run. Once a ball has been bowled and play has come to a stop, the ball is deemed 'dead', and play only resumes when the bowler delivers the next ball. Sometimes a bowler will bowl what is known as an 'illegal delivery'. There are two types:

a) a no-ball (most commonly, when the bowler delivers the ball with their front foot in front of the white line at the end of the pitch, similar to a foot fault in tennis), or

b) a wide (when the ball is bowled out of the batter's reach).

When this happens, a run is added to the batting team's score, and the bowler must bowl another ball. The batter cannot be dismissed from an illegal delivery except by being run out or stumped. So, if a player's stumps are shattered by a delivery that is called a no-ball, the batter will not be given 'out'.

Although we know that the batter is defending three stumps, the bowler will often target an imaginary fourth stump placed outside the batter's off stump. This is to entice the batter to play an attacking shot to score runs. However, if the ball clips the outside edge of their bat, it may well land in the hands of the wicket-keeper or fielders near the wicket-keeper known as slips. The word 'slips' has an interesting origin. It was first mentioned in an early description of the long stop (a fielder behind the wicket keeper), which had to cover many 'slips' made by the batter. The imaginary fourth stump that the bowler aims for is often called the 'corridor of uncertainty' because the batter is unsure whether to go for runs or not, and if they get the edge of their bat on the ball, often it will be caught by one of the slip fielders – meaning the batter will lose their wicket.

The batting team starts their innings with Batter A and Batter B at the wicket. They will bat together in a partnership, accumulating runs for their team, until one, say, Batter B is given out. At that point, Batter B has finished their innings and will trudge glumly back to the Pavilion, to be replaced on the field by Batter C. Batters A and C will then bat together, forming a new partnership until one of them is given out, to be replaced by

Batter D. This process repeats itself until there is only one batter left, meaning that the bowling team has taken ten wickets.

The lone batter will remain 'not out' but the innings will have finished, as they have no more partners to bat with.

A bowler will bowl six deliveries (known collectively as an over) in a row. A bowler cannot bowl two overs consecutively, so after Bowler A bowls the ball six times, they retrieve their hat and sunglasses from the umpire (who chivalrously holds them during the over) and take up a position in the field. Bowler B, who was in the field during the last over, will then bowl the next six balls, but will deliver the ball from the opposite end of the pitch than Bowler A.

Typically, Bowlers A and B will bowl in tandem for a period, alternating overs. Between overs, the fielding team must reassemble so as to face the opposite end of the pitch. Sometimes this natural break is used by the fielding team to discuss tactics. Once the fielding team is in position (usually after 30 to 45 seconds), play resumes.

The fielding team may dismiss batters in a variety of ways. There are actually ten methods, only five of which are common. To signal that a batter is out, the umpire holds their right index finger up in the air. Every wicket is extremely valuable—once you're out, there's no coming back later in the day.

The five most common modes of dismissal (getting out) are as follows:

- **Bowled** – A batter is bowled out if they fail to prevent the ball from crashing into the stumps and at least one of the bails is knocked off. This is by far the most gratifying mode of dismissal for a bowler and the most crushing for a batter. A satisfying and humiliating wooden clunk sound adds to the effect.

- **Caught** - This is self-explanatory. If the ball is caught by a fielder after striking the batter's bat and/or glove and before the ball hits the ground, the batter is out-caught.

- **Stumped** - This is similar to a run-out, where the wicket-keeper throws the ball at the stumps behind the batter after they inadvertently move out of their crease, usually while swinging at and missing the ball.

- **Run out** - This is also fairly self-explanatory. If the batters attempt to run, and the fielding team is able to throw the ball into either of the sets of stumps before the batter can make it to the relevant white line (the crease), that batter is out. The fielding team can either strike the stumps with the ball via a direct hit, or a player can knock off the bails with the hand(s) that is/are holding the ball. Given that running is optional, run-outs generally happen either because one player thought they were fast enough to make it to the other end but was beaten by a fantastic display of fielding or due to miscommunication between the two batters. It is the most frustrating way to get out as it is generally very avoidable!

- **Leg Before Wicket** - The cricketing rule of leg before wicket, or LBW, ranks as one of the more complex rules in all sports! It compares with the difficulty of explaining the rugby or football offside rules. The gist is that a batter is considered out LBW if they obstruct a ball – which would otherwise have hit the stumps - with their pads. Today, umpires have access to technology which not only tracks how the ball travels through the air (like in tennis) but also predicts where the ball would have gone had it not come into contact with the batter or their pads. If the ball had gone on to hit the stumps and it was clear that the batter's pads were in its way, then that batter would be out, lbw.

12. The Main Umpire Signals

If the Umpire decides that a batter is out he will make a signal to everyone concerned to indicate his decision. There are many signals that Umpires use to advise the players, commentators and spectators of their decisions.

The following are the most common:

Six ~ Six runs are scored and awarded to the batter on strike.

Bye ~ When the ball is not a no ball but equally hasn't been hit by the batter, any runs between the wickets that the batter makes, are counted as byes and credited to the team not the batter.

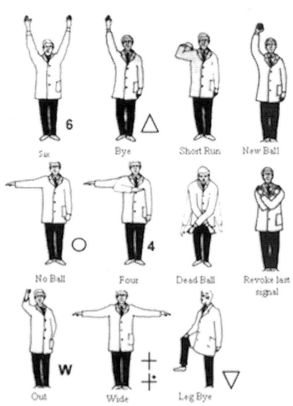

Short Run ~ A run is deemed 'short' when a batter fails to make their ground at either end of the pitch whilst running. Any runs that are 'short' do not count towards the batter's score.

New Ball ~ The new ball has been taken by the fielding side.

No Ball ~ The bowler has made an error when bowling (usually overstepping the line) and needs to bowl the delivery again. One run is added to the batting team total.

Four ~ Four runs are scored and awarded to the batter on strike.

Dead Ball ~ The ball is not in play, so regardless of what happens, the batter cannot be given out, even if they are caught or stumped.

Revoke Last Signal ~ Usually used after a review when the umpire has been advised to overturn their previous decision.

Out ~ The batter is out and must return to the pavilion. The next batter must come in to bat.

Wide ~ The bowler has bowled the ball too wide of the crease and must bowl it again. One run is added to the batting team total.

Leg Bye ~ When the ball is not a no ball and hits the batter on the leg as opposed to their bat, any runs between the wickets that the batter makes, are counted as leg byes and credited to the team not the batter.

13. The Decision Review System (DRS)

Until recently, the sole arbiter of whether a batter was given out rested with the on-field umpires. The umpires (for cost reasons) were usually from the home team which led to some controversial decisions where some captains accused domestic umpires of cheating.

Case in Point

In 1987, a three-match series between Pakistan and England took place in Pakistan. The England captain, Mike Gatting, was miffed with Pakistan umpire Shakoor Rana for wearing a Pakistan sweater during the first match. Despite the touring-team's protests, Rana was chosen to umpire the second Test. In this match, the umpire accused Gatting of cheating, which he strongly denied. In fact, the Pakistan batter, Salim Malik, backed up Gatting. There was a stand-off with the whole of the next days play cancelled, leading to a major diplomatic incident between the two countries. Gatting had to eventually apologise and the match was allowed to resume. The Pakistan Cricket Board wanted to persist with Rana for the third match, but he was eventually replaced.

After this incident, an international panel of recognised umpires was created so that all matches could be officiated by independent umpires.

A fairly recent change is the introduction of the 'DRS' (decision review system), which allows captains to challenge umpiring decisions. Either the batter or the captain of the fielding team has the capacity to challenge the umpire as long as they do so within 15 seconds of the incident. If a decision is challenged, the on-field umpire will refer to the third umpire who is able to access replay and other technology. The third umpire will then make the final decision. If the original umpiring decision is upheld, the team who challenged the decision will lose one of their reviews. If the original umpiring decision is overturned, then the team challenging the decision will retain their review. Each team has three reviews available per inning.

14. Cricket Scoring

This has been mentioned earlier, but I thought it might be helpful to summarise it in one section.

Runs can be scored in several ways:

- By the batting pair running between the stumps after hitting the ball and crossing a line before the bowling side has been able to take the bails off with the ball.

- It doesn't matter whether or not the batter hits the ball (it could ricochet off the pads or, indeed, miss the batter and wicket-keeper). If a run is scored without the ball being hit by the batter, the batting team scores either byes or leg byes, which count equally towards the total.

- If the ball travels outside the playing area (marked out with a boundary rope) but touches the ground on the way, the batting side scores four runs.

- If the ball does not touch the ground on its way over the boundary rope, then the batter scores six runs.

- Extra runs are added should the bowler not bowl a legitimate ball, such as overstepping their mark (a no-ball) or bowling a ball so wide that a batter cannot reasonably reach the ball to hit it (a wide).

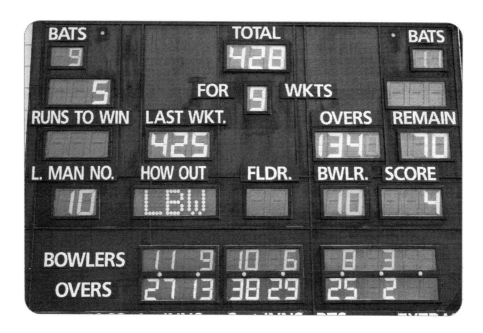

A typical cricket scoreboard contains a huge amount of information. Image above, from left to right and top to bottom, as follows:

Bats: short for Batsman ~ the number 9 tells us that it is the batter at batting position 9 who is batting.

Total: the total run score of the current batting side.

Bats: as above ~ this tells us that the number 11 batter is also currently batting.

Box below Bats: beneath the number 9 is the number 5. This relates to how many runs the batter at number 9 has currently scored.

For 9 Wkts: this tells us how many wickets the batting side has lost. The total here for example is now 428-9 (428 runs and 9 wickets lost).

Overs: this is the number of overs that have been bowled in the innings. The red figure to the right is the number of balls within the over (which will tick round to 6 before the over number increases by 1).

Remain: the number of overs available for the remainder of the day.

L. Man No.: the number of the last batter out - in this case it was the number 10.

How Out: this tells us how the last batter was out - here it was LBW (leg before wicket).

Bowler: this is the number of the bowler who took the last wicket.

Score: this is the run score achieved by the last batter out.

Bowlers: this gives us six numbers which tell us which six bowlers are bowling ~ beneath their number we can see how many overs they have each bowled. Of note, bowler 3 has only bowled 2 overs. This tells us that bowler 3 is likely a part-time bowler who plays higher up the batting order and is therefore considered a batter who can bowl a bit.

33

Throughout an innings, a batting team scores or accumulates runs while the fielding team takes wickets. If, at a certain point, the batting team has scored 72 runs and has lost three wickets, its score is depicted as 72 for 3. If that team scores two runs off the next ball, its score ticks along to 74 for 3 because it has still only lost three wickets but has now scored 74 runs.

If 18 overs have been completed, and a bowler has bowled four balls in the 19th, the number of overs bowled will be represented as 18.4.

The progression goes 18.4, 18.5, 19.0 —i.e., each number after the decimal point represents one ball bowled, not one-tenth of an over.

A player who has scored 30 runs will have a score written as 30* with the asterisk indicating that the batter has not yet been dismissed.

15. Cricket Tactics

Since the teams cannot score runs simultaneously, and teams can score hundreds of runs in each innings, it can be quite difficult to determine which team is winning at any given time. Often, there is no clear answer, with the score bearing little relation to the state of the game. In Test cricket, assessing which team is in a stronger or weaker position will depend on their scores but also crucially on the weather and the condition of the pitch. It is usually not a good idea to try to compare scores until both teams have had a chance to bat. Having said that, if a team is 60 for 8 (60 runs on the board, 8 batters out, 3 left) or 434 for 2 (434 runs on the board, 2 batters out, 9 left), it is fairly clear which one has the upper hand.

Teams attack and defend at different stages during a cricket match. A fielding team looking to take wickets may set an 'attacking field', with more players in catching positions (often behind the wicket or right up close to the batter on strike). If they are trying to keep the batters from scoring, they will adopt a more defensive approach, with fielders spread out away from the bat. In both circumstances, the bowler will adjust their delivery accordingly.

A batter who has just seen several partners get out in quick succession may play defensively in an attempt to conserve their wicket. They may just 'block' the ball rather than take risks by hitting it and attempting to score runs. On the other hand, if the batting team needs to score runs quickly, the batters will swing harder and use creative footwork to work the ball into the gaps in the field. They will also attempt more high-risk running, which increases the chances of them being 'run out'.

The scope for variation in where the ball is bowled and where it is hit is almost infinite: the ball can be delivered to arrive at the batter's feet, knees, chest or head, straight at their body, or in front or behind; and swinging left or right. In general, the height at which the ball will arrive determines whether the batter plays (hits) a front or back foot shot (leaning forward or back to play a shot), while the line of the ball determines in which direction the ball will be played. Naturally, all players have their strengths and weaknesses, and batting and bowling plans are tailored accordingly.

16. Bowling – In More Depth

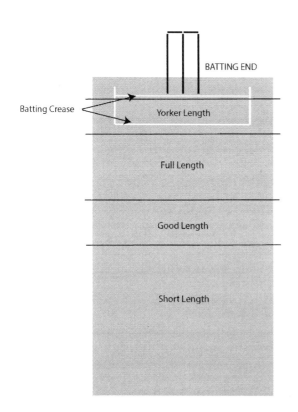

Diagram of Bowling Lengths
(not to scale - illustration purposes only)

A bowler's role:

- To get batters out by taking catches or instigating a run-out.
- To prevent runs from being scored.

Considerations:

- How far up the pitch they want the ball to land (length).
- Which side of the batter do they want it to land, to the batter's left, right or centre (line).

Strategy:

- The bowler, their captain and other senior players will have regular conversations on the pitch to decide where best to place the fielders to achieve the objective of getting the batters out.
- The aim is for the batter to be drawn into playing a shot directly to a fielder or to miss the ball completely; the ball to then knock over the stumps.

- Bowlers will also 'bowl' for LBW dismissals if the batter on strike is particularly weak at 'defending' their stumps.
- A Test Match team usually has five bowlers, one of whom may be an 'all-rounder'– someone who can bowl and bat.
- The captain will rotate the bowlers depending on their skills, who is currently on strike, how many overs each bowler has bowled, and their general fitness, among other considerations.
- Some bowlers are specialist 'new ball' bowlers and will be used to 'open' the bowling for the first few overs, whilst others get results from the balls that are slightly older and softer.
- The positioning of the fielders denotes either an attacking field – placed to engineer and achieve catches – or a defensive field – placed to reduce the runs scored and frustrate the batter.

There are two distinct types of bowling:

i. Fast or pace bowling

ii. Slow or spin bowling

The fielding team will continually rub the ball on their clothing in-between each delivery and new over. This is to 'shine' one side of the ball which allows this side to travel faster through the air. The ball will then be more difficult to bat against as it can spin and swing.

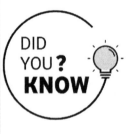

They present different challenges to the batters and require a different skill set:

i. Fast Bowling

This involves the bowler sprinting towards the crease and sending the ball towards the batter at speeds of up to (and sometimes over!) 90 mph. The following terminology applies to these bowlers:

- **Length** – a ball that lands close to the batter, meaning it won't bounce too high, and the batter can readily attack it. If they miss, though, they have an increased chance of being bowled out or caught behind by the wicket-keeper if they 'nick the edge' of their bat onto the ball.

- **Short Ball** – a ball that lands here is likely to climb higher and reach the batter between their ribcage and their head. If the batter is able to connect with this delivery, the pace and height will allow them to readily score runs, however when the ball is coming towards their head at close to 90mph, it's not uncommon for the batter to duck out of the way.

- **Yorker** – this is a ball that lands right at the batsman's feet – a bit like when a golf ball lands in a bunker. It is virtually impossible for the batter to hit this normally; they have to try to scoop beneath it or get out of the way. This is a very effective ball to bowl as often it can be knocked onto the wicket or create an LBW dismissal. However, it is a risky strategy because the bowler has to be inch-perfect when landing the ball.

- **Swing** – the fielding team will continually 'shine' one side of the ball on their clothing and this is to give the ball a 'swing' trajectory when bowled. See 'Did You Know' below.

ii. Spin Bowling

- Spin bowlers have a standard ball that makes up most of their deliveries. For an off-spinner, this is usually the off-break; for a leg spinner, it is usually the leg break.

- An off-break means that the ball lands and then moves to the right as the bowler looks towards a right-handed batter. A leg break is the opposite.
- They will bowl their stock ball repeatedly, with slight variations in flight, line, and length, to get the batter into a rhythm and then break it up with a variation such as an arm ball for an off-spinner or a googly for a leg spinner (in both cases the ball turns in the opposite direction to the bowlers' stock ball). If a batter does not pick the variation, the different spin and bounce of the ball can cause them to lose their wicket. Good spin bowlers can be dangerous to bat defensively against, as they will usually have close fielders near to the batter to catch the ball if it flies into the air, even if it's only a few yards from the bat.

Spinners pitch the ball closer to the batter than fast bowlers because:

- It gives the ball more time in the air before it lands, which deceives the batter
- The batter has less time to react after the ball bounces because it is so much closer to them.
- There are often scuff marks on the pitch close to the batter caused by the bowlers running in from the other end. These scuff marks can be a great place to 'land' a spin ball because its ongoing trajectory will be difficult to predict.

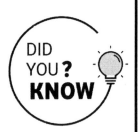

DID YOU ? KNOW

A 'maiden' is the name given to an over in which the batter has not scored any runs. 'Maiden' means 'unmarried' or 'previously untouched'. An over without runs is a 'virgin' over, hence the term 'maiden' was coined.

- A spinner may tempt the batter to come onto the front foot and then advance down the pitch by pitching balls shorter. If the batter has advanced down the pitch, they are likely to be outside of their batting crease, so if they miss the ball and it goes through to the wicket-keeper, they stand every chance of being stumped out.

Choosing Bowlers

There is a rule stating that bowlers are not permitted to bowl two successive overs, which means the captain must decide which bowlers to use and when. Bowlers will form a partnership in the same way as batters; one will bowl from each end.

The bowler chosen depends on several factors:

- How many overs have already been bowled with that particular ball.
- The relative skills of the available bowlers in the side.
- The styles of the bowlers available.
- The freshness or tiredness of bowlers.
- Whether a bowler has been performing well or poorly in the game so far.
- The state of the pitch and whether it has deteriorated over the course of the game.

- Any known strengths or weaknesses of the batters to particular bowlers or styles of bowling.
- The state of the game and overall strategic position – is it more important to take wickets or prevent runs being scored?
- The temperature and humidity.

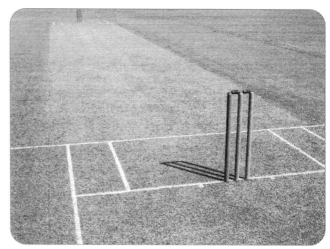

The age of the ball:

- Fast bowlers obtain greater bounce and movement with a newer ball and usually bowl the first 20-25 overs of a Test match innings.
- The attack is opened by the side's best two fast bowlers, with these being changed every 5-10 overs depending on conditions.
- If the ball is getting old, a spin bowler can achieve significant spin from the cracks and deviations in the pitch surface. It is usual for spinners to bowl later in the game, and if the light is poor so that the batter is not facing super-fast deliveries in fading light.
- In Test match cricket, the balls are changed either every 80 overs or more frequently if they are damaged.
- When the 80-over mark is reached, it is the captain's decision whether to replace the ball. Sometimes, this is delayed if a spinner is achieving great results with the ball, for example, but more often than not, the ball is changed within ten overs of the 80 mark.

Bowling over or around the wicket

When a bowler (fast or slow) runs in towards the batter, they can deliver the ball with the stumps to their left or right. If they decide to have the stumps on their right (for a right-handed bowler), they are said to be bowling 'over' the wicket. If they choose to bowl with the stumps to the left, they are bowling 'around' the wicket. Bowlers usually choose to bowl over the wicket, as this means their bowling arm is close to the middle of the pitch. Bowlers will only switch to around the wicket for particular tactical reasons, usually to provide variation when a batter is proving hard to dislodge.

17. Batting – In More Depth

A big part of batting in cricket is judging which deliveries to play and which ones to leave alone. Steering the ball accurately between fielders is also a key skill. Whilst it may seem obvious for a batter to just hit everything, that's not necessarily the best method. One mistake is all it takes for them to lose their wicket, so batters learn to be selective in the balls they hit – especially in Test match cricket.

A ball that is old (used) or wet will behave differently to one that is new, shiny and dry.

Batting Order

The order in which a team bats is usually determined by the abilities of the batters. A typical side will have 6 specialist batters, a wicket-keeper and four specialist bowlers. Two of the batters will be specialist openers (who start the innings). They have the experience and skills required to bat when the ball is brand new and tends to swing and bounce more. This is a demanding task, and batting generally gets easier as the ball gets older. These openers will bat at positions 1 and 2, beginning the innings together. They will not necessarily be the best batters in the side but those who are most experienced at opening the innings. Positions 3 to 6 will be filled by the remaining specialist batters, usually in order of batting ability. Thus, the number 3 batter is usually the best batter in the side.

Position 7 will usually be held by the wicket-keeper. Historically, wicket-keepers were poorer batters than some or even all the bowlers and batted correspondingly lower in the order. In modern times, wicket-keepers are selected as much for their batting as their ability to keep wicket. Occasionally, wicket-keepers can be better at batting than some of the specialist batters, however, they will still bat lower down the order so they have sufficient rest time in between keeping wicket (which is incredibly demanding) and batting. Positions 8 to 11 will be occupied by the bowlers, again in order from best to poorest batting ability.

The reason the side is arranged from best to poorest batting ability is to allow the best batters to play earlier in the team's innings and, in theory, bat longer due to their level of skill. Thus, maximising the score.

Changing the Batting Order

The batting order can be changed at any time during a match for various reasons, such as:

- The most dangerous time for a batter, in terms of the likelihood of getting out, is at the start of their innings, before getting used to the light, pace, movement and bounce of the ball. This also applies at the start of a day or session. Therefore, if a wicket falls and a batter has to begin their innings late in the day, say, they will end up having to 'start' their innings twice. In this situation, if the next batter due in is a specialist batter, the captain may opt to send a lower-order player out instead to protect the specialist batter. This is known as a night watchman.

- If a side wants to score runs quickly to have a good chance of winning, the captain may switch the batting line-up by promoting a player based on their ability to score runs quickly instead of one who may be more skilful but slower to score.

> If a batter is given out without scoring, they are said to have been out for a **duck**. If they are out first ball, they are said to have been out for a **golden duck**. The reason it's called a duck is because the shape of a duck's egg is oval, like the number 0.

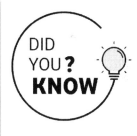

DID YOU **?** **KNOW**

- It can be advantageous if they have both a right and left-handed batter in play at the same time. This can be inconvenient for the fielding side who will need to change their fielding positions more often and the bowler will also have to change their action and direction of the ball. This can lead to frustration for the fielding side.

Shot Selection

When on strike, a batter can decide to:

- Not play at the ball – deeming it too risky
- Play a defensive shot – respecting that a quality ball has been delivered

- Play an attacking shot – seeing a valuable opportunity to score runs
- Actively evade the ball – if it is heading for their body or head

Their decision as to what shot to play is influenced by several factors. A **defensive** shot may be played due to:

- It being near the beginning of the match
- They have just started their innings
- They are playing against a new ball
- Facing a skilful bowler or one who has been performing well in the current game
- The pitch is deteriorating, with uneven bounce and pace
- Facing a bowling style with which the batter is less comfortable
- Being unable to confidently determine the type of ball being bowled
- If their team is unable to realistically score enough runs to win the match in the time remaining, so they are holding out for a draw
- Close to the end of a session or day's play
- Instructions from the captain to bat defensively

The following situations will tend to encourage a batter to play **attacking** shots:

- Being settled in
- Playing against an old ball
- Facing a poor bowler or one who is performing poorly
- The pitch is playing well, with consistent bounce and pace
- Facing a bowling style with which the batter is comfortable
- Being able to confidently pick the type of ball being bowled
- When there are few or no fielders close to the bat
- The side is looking for runs to be scored quickly in order to win
- Instructions from the captain to bat aggressively

Each batter will consistently update their strategy throughout the game, depending on how they are playing and the current state of the match.

Sharing the Strike

With two good batters playing together (or, in cricket slang, 'at the crease'), it doesn't matter which one faces any particular ball. They will score runs whenever they can, and swap ends when they happen to score one or three runs. They tend to like swapping ends rather than remaining at one end for long since it means the bowlers need to adjust to bowling to a different batter every few balls. This can be especially true if one batter is right-handed and the other left-handed, since the bowling line to attack each will be different.

The situation changes when enough wickets fall so that a relatively poor batter comes in to bat with the remaining good one. In this situation, it is tactically better if the better player takes most of the strike. To do this, the better batter may not take one or three runs even if they are available, restricting them to twos or boundaries during the first half of the over. Depending on how confident the batter is in their partner, the better players will try to score 1 or 3 on the 4th, 5th, or 6th ball of an over. This gives them the strike again at the start of the next over. This tactic is known as farming the strike.

18. The End of an Innings – Declarations & Following On

Declaring

As mentioned earlier, in order to win a Test Match, a team needs to bowl out the opposition twice. If a team bats too long (say more than two days), the captain may feel that there is not enough time to dismiss the opposition twice and hence not win the match. In this situation, the captain may decide to forfeit the rest of an innings, which is known as declaring. The score is then given as 650 for 3 dec. (for example), meaning that the team have declared with a score of 650 for the loss of only 3 wickets.

The basic strategy behind declaring is to consider this when you think you have enough runs to win the match. The captain will weigh up how many runs have been scored by each side so far, the condition of the pitch and how much time is left to play the game. This can be complicated by the prospect of adverse weather, which can potentially use up playing time.

Most first inning declarations occur in the last hour or so of play on day two. This is because the most dangerous time for new batters is when they are at the start of their innings. Forcing the other side to bat for a short time near the end of a day's play and then having to start again the following morning is incredibly challenging and maximises the potential for wickets to be taken by the fielding team.

Captains may also decide to declare after their second (and the matches' third innings). This is to provide their own side with enough time to bowl out the opposing side in the last innings of a match and thus win the game. The first Test match between Pakistan and England in Rawalpindi in 2022 was heading for a draw, with both sides having made big scores in their first innings. However, the England captain bravely declared on the fourth day, leaving Pakistan to chase 343 with a day and a half to go. The hosts were 80/2 by the end of day four and were well-placed going into the fifth and final day. Unfortunately for Pakistan, the next day, they collapsed to 268 all out in the final hour of the fifth and final day as England took a 1-0 series lead.

Following On

Imagine the situation where the team batting first posts a significant score, let's say 546 (either all out or by choosing to declare an innings closed early). The opposing team will have been in the field for many hours and will be exhausted mentally and physically. They then come out to bat and will be trying to score a similar number of runs but their first goal is to score enough runs to avoid what is known as the 'follow on'. If a team is dismissed with a greater than 200 run deficit to their opponents, the opposing captain can insist the team follow on, which means bat again. In this instance, they will bat their two innings back-to-back, which is a huge mental task.

However, enforcing the follow-on also means that the captain's side will have to field for two consecutive innings without resting in between, which is not always a good situation for them. The bowlers and wicket-keeper, in particular, might need recovery time.

19. Fielding in Summary

- All eleven fielding players will be on the pitch for the duration of their opponent's innings.
- They will collect the ball (from where it has landed after being hit) and return it to the bowler and/or wicket-keeper. They will also attempt to catch the ball so that they can dismiss a player.
- If they stop the ball from going over the boundary rope, they can also save runs by collecting it and getting it back to the wicket quickly, which means the batters won't be able to run between the wickets as many times.

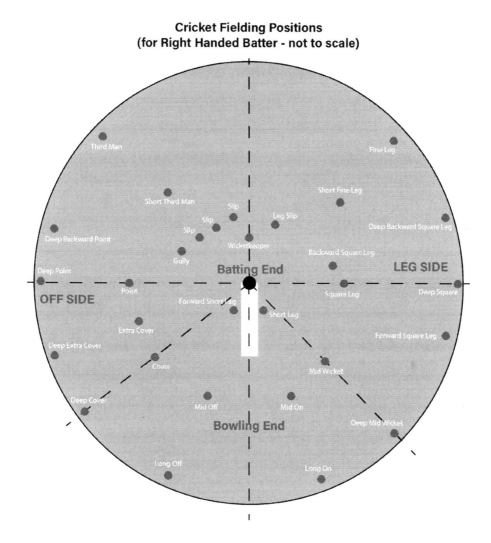

Cricket Fielding Positions
(for Right Handed Batter - not to scale)

Generally, captains stick to set field placings:

- Slip fielders are on the offside and in line with where the ball will travel if it is edged off the bat. There can be up to four fielders in the slips, referred to as a slip cordon.
- Gully stands to the side of the slips.
- Point fielders are in line with the batter on the offside. This is referred to as 'square' of the wicket. Backward point is a variation of this.

- Mid-off is a much-used fielding position close to the bowler.
- Mid-on is the same as mid-off but on the other side of the bowler.
- Square Leg is in line with the batter and wicket, on the opposite side of the pitch to the Point fielder. There is often an umpire positioned at square leg.
- Boundary fielders are those who stand just inside the boundary ropes. Sometimes they are referred to as boundary riders.

20. The Ashes

Cricket is a very popular sport in many countries. There are several important series where competing teams face off, such as the matches between India and Pakistan. In those countries, everything stops when cricket matches are being played. For Test matches, the rivalry between Australia and England is something very special, and these two teams play in an exclusive tournament known as **The Ashes**.

The Ashes originated in 1882 as a result of a satirical obituary published in an English newspaper called The Sporting Times. This 'obituary' was published following a cricket match at The Oval in London, where Australia beat England on English soil for the first time.

The newspaper announced the 'death of English cricket' and stated that the body would be cremated, with the ashes taken to Australia. The English media referred to the next English tour to Australia (1882-83) as the quest to regain The Ashes, and during this tour, a group of women from Melbourne gifted a small terracotta urn to the England captain, Ivo Bligh. It is believed that the urn contains the ashes of one or two of the bails used in the match.

AI Representation

21. Cricketing Greats

There have been so many great cricketers over the years, but one stands out above the rest. The Australian Sir Donald Bradman, known to many Aussies as simply 'the Don', averaged 99.94 runs across the 52 Test Matches he played for Australia between 1928 and 1948. It's one of the greatest sporting records of all time: no other batsman who has played more than 20 Tests has come anywhere close.

In his last match, Bradman walked out to the crease needing to score just four runs to achieve an astonishing career average of 100 in Test cricket. Unfortunately, he was dismissed for a second-ball duck.

Other notable greats:

- **Steve Smith**, **Ricky Ponting** and **Shane Warne** have been among Australia's best players in recent years.
- India has produced both **Sachin Tendulkar** (known affectionately as the 'little master') and **Virat Kohli**, two of the best batsmen of their time.
- **Sir Viv Richards** of the West Indies is regarded as one of the best batsmen of all time and had a nickname of the 'master blaster'.
- **Sir Jack Hobbs** nicknamed 'The Master', averaged 57 runs across his 61 Tests for England. Two other notables for England are **WG Grace** and **Ian Botham**.
- Pakistan, Sri Lanka and South Africa have all had world-class players such as **Wasim Akram**, **Mahela Jayawardena** and **Jacques Kallis**.

22. Superstitions

Like many who play sport, cricketers can be a superstitious bunch. One famous superstition is known as **Nelson**, and it refers to a score of 111. This is also used for multiples of 111, such as 222 (double Nelson), 333 (triple Nelson), and so on. It can apply to an individual player or the team as a whole.

The Nelson score is considered unlucky because the number 111 is similar in appearance to a wicket without a bail. Players and fans believed something bad or unlucky would occur when a player or team reached that score – but why is it called Nelson? It is widely believed that Lord Nelson's injuries are the reason for this.

Famous cricket historian Bill Frindall once referred to the occurrence of this score as Nelson because:

"Horatio Nelson had lost his one eye, one arm, and one etcetera in the war".

Among Australian players and fans, the score considered unlucky is 87. They call it the Devil's number because 87 deducted from 100 is 13.

23. Amusing Quotes and Sledging

Amusing quotes (from some well-known commentators):

Brian Johnston
"The Bowler's Holding, the batsman's Willey."

In this case, West Indian fast bowler Michael Holding was bowling to England's Peter Willey. It's widely felt that Johnners was deliberately mischievous.

Trevor Bailey
"Logie decided to chance his arm, and it came off."

Meaning Logie took a risk that paid off.

Jonathan Agnew
"He couldn't quite get his leg over."

Agnew claims the quote, made famous by co-commentator Brian Johnston, who couldn't speak for laughing in the aftermath, was an 'accidental' gaffe.

Sledging (words directed at opposing players on the pitch, usually to intimidate them):

- **Sir Viv Richards v Greg Thomas**

Whilst playing for Somerset, Sir Viv Richards produced a legendary retort. After playing and missing (attempting to hit the ball but failing to do so) at successive deliveries, Glamorgan bowler Greg Thomas made the brave decision to give Viv some verbal as to the appearance of the ball.

"It's red, round and weighs about five ounces, in case you were wondering."

Of course, the next ball was launched out of the ground by the West Indian legend accompanied by the following words.

"Greg, you know what it looks like, now go and find it."

- **Daryll Cullinan v Shane Warne**

The late Australian spin bowler Shane Warne quipped to South African batter Daryll Cullinan as he made his way to the crease: "I've been waiting four years for another chance to humiliate you".

Cullinan responded, "It looks like you spent it eating".

- **Eddo Brandes v Glenn McGrath**

After Zimbabwean Eddo Brandes played and missed a Glenn McGrath delivery, the towering Aussie bowler enquired: "Oi, Brandes, why are you so fat?"

The immediacy of Brandes' reply had Aussies Ricky Ponting and Michael Clarke in stitches: "Because every time I sleep with your wife, she gives me a biscuit".

- **Ian Botham v Rod Marsh**

The England player Ian Botham came out to bat and was greeted by the following comment from the Australian wicket-keeper, "So, how's your wife and my kids?"

Botham struck back with a witty line of his own.

"The wife is fine, but the kids are retarded."

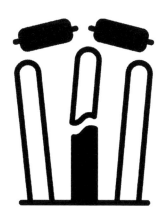

Chapter Two

FORMULA ONE

"A lot of people criticise Formula One as an unnecessary risk. But what would life be like if we only did what was necessary?"

Niki Lauda

CONTENTS

1. What is Formula 1?

Formula 1 is a motorsport in which 20 drivers compete over 24 races worldwide to win the World Championship. Teams (with two drivers) work to produce some of the most powerful, technologically advanced cars in the world. Drivers who finish in the top ten of the race earn points for themselves and their teams. The drivers and teams aim is to earn the most points by the season's end.

The race winner receives 25 points, and the driver in tenth place receives 1 point. These points are added to the individual driver's total as well as to the overall team score, meaning that each team has three different totals: one for each driver individually and one combined driver total, which is known as the 'constructors' total. It is, therefore, possible for the Team to win the Constructors Championship without either of their drivers winning the Drivers' Championship. Similarly, a driver can win the Driver's Championship without the team necessarily winning the constructors championship.

The term 'Formula' refers to a strict set of rules followed by the car's constructors, mechanics, and drivers. 'One' comes from the grading that The Federation Internationale de l'Automobile (FIA) issues to the race tracks, cars and driver licences. Formula One is governed by the FIA, which was set up in 1904 as a non-profit (yes, really) organisation that the Formula One Group owns.

In the early days of motor racing, there were no restrictions on the size or power of the cars, which inevitably led to unfair advantages for those with larger and more powerful vehicles. This also posed significant risks for the participants, which resulted in many severe injuries and fatalities. Following World War II, the FIA implemented regulations to level the playing field for drivers by limiting the size and power of the cars. This shift placed greater emphasis on car efficiency, design and driver skill and the organisation now closely monitors and modifies Formula One rules for driver safety, fair play and fan satisfaction.

DID YOU? KNOW

Typically it costs about $12 million to build a Formula One car!

2. Equipment

- Drivers must wear helmets, shoes, gloves, HANS devices (Head and Neck Support) and race suits specifically designed for F1 races.
- The HANS Device system was introduced in 2003 and consists of a carbon fibre shoulder collar which is secured under the driver's safety belts and is connected to their helmet by two elastic straps.
- The cars (as of 2023) are not allowed to be more than 5.63 meters (18 ½ feet) long, 2 meters (6 foot 6 inches) wide, and 95 cm (3 feet) high.
- Teams were allowed to spend up to $135m on the cars in the 2023 season.
- In 2019, teams transported more than 1,000 tonnes of equipment from race to race. Bigger teams usually take around 100 people and 50 tonnes of cargo to each race!

3. History

The 'modern' era of Formula One began in 1950, but its original roots go back a lot further. In fact, it is possible to trace racing back to the 1890s when road races took place in France. Originally, cars were upright and heavy; roads were made of sand or wood; reliability was non-existent; drivers were accompanied by mechanics and races (usually on public roads from town to town) were seriously long. The first proper race was a 1,200 km (750 miles) road race from Paris to Bordeaux in 1895. It was won in 48 hours (bear in mind that most modern Grand Prix races are no more than two hours) at an average speed of just 25kmph.

In 1901, the first race that took the 'Grand Prix' moniker was hosted at Le Mans in France. It was won by Ferencz Szisz in a Renault, who drove the 1,120 kilometres (700 miles) at an average speed of 100 kph (62.5 mph). In six years, the speed had therefore increased, but it was significantly slower than the speeds achieved by modern F1 cars. Seven years later, pits appeared for the first time in a race in Sicily. These were dug by the side of the track and were a place where mechanics could work.

In 1931, the International Grand Prix was formed, and because (at that time) all of the races took place in Europe, the championship became known as the European Automobile Championship. This was the first international drivers' championship in motor racing history. The original regulations stipulated a

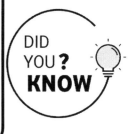

Early F1 cars became too heavy and fast for their tyres which meant mechanics had to regularly replace them. The winning Mercedes in the 1908 French Grand Prix in Dieppe, shredded ten tyres!

DID YOU **?** KNOW

time of ten hours for the races as opposed to a finite distance. Due to this, each car had two drivers who took turns. At the time, there were no limits on the engine size or the weight of the cars, and the winner was simply the pair who had completed the longest distance in the allotted ten hours.

In 1934, factory teams from Auto Union (now Audi) and Mercedes-Benz emerged, with massive financial support from the Third Reich on Adolph Hitler's orders. These beautiful and powerful German cars first introduced aerodynamics into Grand Prix car design, which, as we now know, is one of the most crucial elements of the modern Formula One car.

After the Second World War, the minimum race distance was reduced to 300 km (186 miles); on 10 April 1950, Juan Manuel Fangio, in a Maserati, won the French Grand Prix in Pau. This was the first race to be called an 'International Formula One' race.

In the past, F1 teams like McLaren-Renault were named after the two companies who collaborated to build the car. McLaren was responsible for the chassis, whilst Renault supplied the engine, so together, they aimed to create a car suitable for their drivers and the race tracks.

As of Australia 2024, F1 has seen a total of 1,104 races taking place in 34 different countries. This equates to 73 seasons in which 34 drivers from 15 nationalities have won the drivers' championship.

Germany's Michael Schumacher and Britain's Lewis Hamilton jointly hold the record for the most world championships with each winning seven driver's titles. Lewis Hamilton was controversially denied an eighth championship win in 2021 during a last lap, final race decider with Holland's Max Verstappen. Opinion remains divided as to the validity of the outcome of this race and, ultimately, the championship; however, despite many enquiries and some senior heads rolling, the result stands (this is covered in more detail later). Max Verstappen has since gone on to win two more driver titles, whilst Ferrari currently holds the constructor's record with a total of 16 constructor's titles.

4. Notable Landmarks

1933 Starting positions on the grid were decided by qualifying times for the first time at the Monaco Grand Prix.

1946 Formula One was agreed as a recognised formula.

1950 The drivers' world championship was launched, with the first race being the British Grand Prix at Silverstone on 13 May 1950.

1958 The first constructors' championship was launched.

1958 The practice of sharing cars during a race was banned.

1958 Rule changes included reducing the length of races from 500km or three hours to 300km or two hours (which remains to this day).

1968 Lotus cars carried Imperial Tobacco logos on their cars, heralding the arrival of sponsorship. The FIA banned tobacco advertising in 2006.

1977 Renault produced the first turbocharged car, which was eventually banned in 1989.

1978 Medical cars were introduced to follow cars on the formation lap of every Grand Prix. **On its first-ever appearance, the medical car hit a kerb and lifted off into the air!**

1982 A drivers strike took place ahead of the South African Grand Prix, protesting against the introduction of driver's licences.

1994 Ayrton Senna was killed at the San Marino Grand Prix, one day after Roland Ratzenberger also lost his life in an accident during qualifying. These two tragedies led to a drive for the improvement of safety standards. Though they were technically the last drivers to die at the wheel of their car, Jules Bianchi crashed into one of the recovery cranes on the final lap of the Japanese Grand Prix in 2014 and, having survived the initial impact, later died in hospital from his injuries.

5. The Cars

Formula One is primarily focused on the cars, which are remarkable feats of engineering and require a significant amount of work to build. Over the years, Formula One cars have undergone tremendous changes to minimise the risk to drivers and increase the sport's appeal for spectators. Today's cars are safer and more agile; improved dynamics and the incorporation of electronics have given drivers better control over the vehicles, resulting in faster speeds and fewer accidents.

Despite this, Formula 1 cars still retain considerable risk with a single driver seated in an open cockpit (the HALO device is a recent addition – think roll bar - but the cockpit is still essentially open).

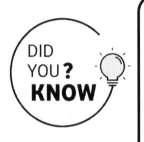

Formula One cars reach a speed greater than that of an aeroplane at take-off.

On take-off, a plane reaches 240-285 kph, whilst an F1 car can reach speeds of up to 350 kph!

Minimum Weight of the Cars

When I started investigating the weight issue, I assumed (wrongly) that each car's permitted weight limit would be a maximum rather than a minimum. Still, I have since understood that teams want their cars to be as light as possible to achieve the fastest pace. Hence, the limit applied by the FIA is a minimum.

Initially, the minimum weight requirement for F1 cars was 795kg. However, manufacturers needed help meeting this requirement, so it was subsequently increased by 3kg. A later proposal to reduce the weight limit by 2kg was not implemented; consequently, the current weight limit for F1 cars remains at 798 kilograms.

Considering the added weight of new mandatory electronic items and heavier tyres, this has become challenging. Not least because this limit must also include the weight of the driver, but not the fuel. The fuel weight is allowed on top of the 798kg and is set at a maximum of 110kg. Therefore, at the beginning of a Grand Prix, each car can weigh close to 1,000kg.

After the race, each car and driver are weighed to ensure that the minimum weight of 798kg has been adhered to, taking into account the weight of any fuel not burned during the race. Some cars manufactured below the weight limit will often add ballast to ensure that the weight restrictions are complied with.

Car Design

Formula One cars are aerodynamically designed to minimise resistance to air. This feature helps them attain incredible speeds, consume less fuel, and get a better grip on the tarmac.

> A jet engine produces 30 brake horsepower when cruising. The brake horsepower of an F1 car is 1,000!

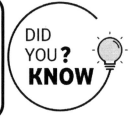

DID YOU **?** **KNOW**

The cars have diffusers at the rear, which create downforce by allowing air to flow underneath. On average, a Formula One car produces 5G of downforce, which is five times the weight of the car pressing down on the track. This downforce provides the necessary traction for the tyres and prevents the car from skidding on bends and sharp corners. The result of achieving this level of downforce is that drivers can navigate corners and bends at much higher speeds than road cars.

6. The Engines

First things first, a modern F1 engine is no longer called an engine; it is referred to as a 'power unit'. This is because it's a hybrid. The vehicle is powered by a petrol engine and electric motors, supported by an Energy Recovery System (ERS). When these were first introduced in 2014, many criticised ERS for their lack of noise compared to the popular ear-splitting V8 and V10 monsters of days gone by. Though they might lack the noise, these new engines are the most powerful and efficient in Grand Prix history.

A system known as KERS (Kinetic Energy Recovery System) forms part of the ERS System, which allows the heat lost when the driver brakes (kinetic energy) to be recovered and stored in the battery for later use. Essentially, KERS is an energy-saving system that converts wasted kinetic energy into electrical energy.

How much horsepower does an F1 power unit produce?

The power of an engine is measured in horsepower. One brake horsepower is equal to the amount of energy needed to lift an object weighing 15,000 Kg (the weight of many family cars) by one foot in one minute.

The total power output from the combined petrol and electric elements is around 1,000 brake horsepower (bhp). This is significantly higher than a standard road car; even the DB7 driven by James Bond doesn't reach 300 bhp. Also, an F1 car can cover 0 to 60mph in around 2.6 seconds and has a top speed of around 360 kph (225 mph).

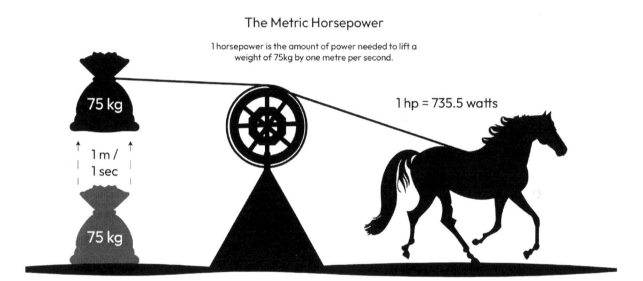

The above picture (apart from looking pretty) shows that 1 horsepower (hp) is the amount of power needed to lift a weight of 75kg by one metre per second. One metric horsepower is approximately equivalent to 735.5 watts.

As previously mentioned, the engines used in F1 cars changed in 2014, and they are all now equipped with 1.6 litre V6 turbocharged engines. For those unfamiliar with this terminology (such as me!), the number following the 'V' indicates the number of cylinders in the engine, whilst the number preceding the 'L' refers to the engine's displacement volume in litres, which ultimately determines the engine size.

The above picture (apart from looking pretty) shows that 1 horsepower (hp) is the amount of power needed to lift a weight of 75kg by one metre per second. One metric horsepower is approximately equivalent to 735.5 watts.

7. Tyres

Tyres are a crucial component of Formula One cars. Unlike those on street cars, Formula One tyres are built to last between 60 and 120 kilometres (40 to 80 miles) only. Imagine having to change your tyres every 60 miles. Given that the shortest road distance from London to Edinburgh is roughly 378 miles, you'd need to stop seven times to change your tyres if you were journeying in an F1 car!

Pirelli introduced a new range of 18-inch tyres for 2023, consisting of six dry compounds: C0, C1, C2, C3, C4, and C5, as well as intermediates and full wets to cater to various weather conditions.

To select the appropriate tyre, Pirelli will choose three compounds from the C0-C5 range, considering the characteristics of the track and climate. The hardest trio will be selected for tracks that demand more from the tyres, while the softest will be chosen for those that require less.

During the race weekend, the highest-numbered tyre will be marked red and referred to as the soft, the middle compound will be marked yellow and referred to as the medium, and the lowest-numbered tyre will be marked white and referred to as the hard. The green intermediate and blue full-wet tyres will also be available.

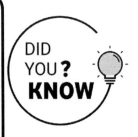

All Formula One cars have to use tyres produced by the same manufacturer.

Currently, the Italian brand Pirelli produces all of the tyres for F1 cars in a deal that is due to last until 2027.

Soft tyres are often called 'slicks' and are used to achieve the fastest pace. However, they degrade (wear out) faster than the other compounds, meaning more pit stops to change them. The wet tyre is the slowest but critical when the race is run in wet conditions. If a driver uses slick or medium tyres during wet races, they will lose grip and almost certainly slide off the track. Therefore, teams and their drivers must carefully consider the expected weather conditions for the whole race. If they believe that rain will only fall for the first five or ten minutes of a race, they may use 'dry weather tyres' throughout to save an additional pit stop.

8. The Season

A Formula One season consists of several races and usually runs from March to December.

At the end of the season, the World Drivers' Championship and the Constructors' Championship are awarded to the winners. The drivers' championship is decided by the cumulative number of points a driver has won during the season, and the Constructors' Championship is awarded to the team with the highest number of points accumulated by both drivers during the season.

Points are awarded to drivers and teams based on where they finish in a race.

- The winner receives 25 points.
- The second-place finisher 18 points.
- The driver finishing third receives 15 points.
- The fourth-placed driver receives 12 points.
- Fifth to tenth place receive 10, 8, 6, 4, 2 and 1 points, respectively.

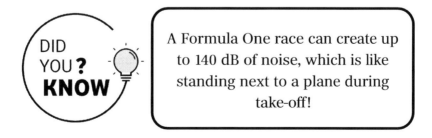

DID YOU ? KNOW

A Formula One race can create up to 140 dB of noise, which is like standing next to a plane during take-off!

9. The Teams

It's not widely known amongst casual observers, but Formula One is referred to as a team sport because it involves hundreds of technicians, engineers and support staff. Each of the ten teams competing in the 2024 season employs around a thousand individuals, including designers and assembly workers. A Formula One team owns the intellectual rights for everything it produces within its team; thus, if the chassis is designed by one company and another supplies the engine, they will both fall under the 'umbrella' of the team, and their expertise can be combined to create one team and name, for example, Benetton-Ford and Williams-Renault.

Some teams employ 'team orders', meaning their senior driver can overtake the more junior driver during a race if it is to the team and driver's advantage. In this instance, the junior driver will potentially sacrifice their own individual points, which demonstrates that despite every driver racing for themselves, it is also very much a team sport. This is less prevalent now than it was. Still, if there is a chance of one driver winning the world championship, for example, then it isn't unheard of for their teammate to 'assist' by potentially 'holding up' their closest rival – within the scope of the FIA rules, of course!

10. The Drivers

Here is the list of F1 teams for 2024, along with their drivers:

- **Mercedes** with *Lewis Hamilton* and *George Russell*
- **Red Bull Racing** with *Max Verstappen* and *Sergio Perez*
- **Ferrari** with *Charles Leclerc* and *Carlos Sainz*
- **McLaren** with *Lando Norris* and *Oscar Piastri*
- **Alpine F1 Team** with *Esteban Ocon* and *Pierre Gasly*
- **Visa Cash App RB Team** with *Yuki Tsunoda* and *Daniel Ricciardo*
- **Aston Martin** with *Fernando Alonso* and *Lance Stroll*
- **Williams** with *Alexander Albon* and *Logan Sargeant*
- **Alfa Romeo Racing** with *Valtteri Bottas* and *Guanyu Zhou*
- **Haas F1 Team** with *Kevin Magnussen* and *Nico Hulkenberg*

It is normal for drivers to switch teams on a reasonably regular basis. Some drivers will stay with their teams for a considerable length of time, though, if they have a good relationship and have achieved great results. If the driver is not satisfied with the team or car, though, or the team doesn't think they have the right driver, changes will be made. Usually, these changes are made during the off-season, although it is not unheard of for a driver change to be made mid-season if necessary. Formula One teams will have many 'test' drivers available who can stand in at a moment's notice.

The driver line-up has been stable for the last couple of seasons (2023, 2024); however, Lewis Hamilton recently announced that he is leaving Mercedes at the end of this season (having won six of his World titles with them) to drive for Ferrari next season (2025). This will mean an inevitable shake-up through the rest of the field, and what is known as the 'driver merry-go-round' has started in preparation for the 2025 season.

Formula One drivers are as fit as most athletes in any sport—sometimes fitter. They must have exceptional stamina and excellent reflexes because driving a Formula One car is physically and mentally demanding. Drivers dedicate a lot of time during the season and off-season to maintaining their physical health and well-being. They know that every time they get in their cars, they put their lives on the line and need to be in the best shape to minimise these risks.

As mentioned earlier, drivers lose a lot of weight during a race due in no small part to the amount of energy expended when countering the G force on bends and sharp corners. Drivers will experience a force of 2G when accelerating and a force of up to 6G on a sharp corner. Although a driver's body is firmly strapped into their seat, their necks and legs are free to move. Keeping their legs and neck in position under these high G forces takes a lot of strength and effort, which is why F1 drivers prioritise strengthening their neck muscles.

A Formula One driver typically loses 3 kg of weight during a race. This is about the weight of a standard house brick.

11. Drivers Rule(s)!

- They must have an F1 super licence – an ordinary driving licence is insufficient. *
- They must be at least 18 years old.
- They must choose (and stick to) a race number. Only a reigning world champion can change their race number to 1 following their winning season.
- Full race gear must be worn during practice, qualifying and the actual race.
- Drivers cannot talk to their teammates during the race but can communicate with their team.
- Drivers have to brake with their left foot as there is not enough space (in the cockpit) for a right-foot brake pedal.
- They have to participate in random drug testing.

*Like us mere mortals, F1 drivers can incur penalties for on-course incidents. They will receive a one-race ban if they accumulate 12 points on their licence.

12. The Circuits

A circuit usually begins with a straight stretch followed by several bends and corners. Most circuits run clockwise; however, the few that run anticlockwise give the drivers additional trouble. The G force on their necks is now pushing in the opposite direction to what they are used to.

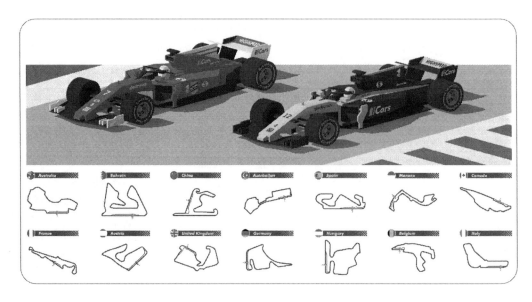

A representation of circuits on the F1 calendar

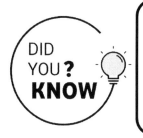
There are three main circuit types used in Formula One today:

i.   The most common is the **proper circuit**. Tracks like Silverstone, Monza, the Hungaroring and the Circuit of the Americas are designed and built specifically for racing.

ii. The second type is the **street circuit**. For these races, public roads are closed off for the racing event. The Grand Prix at Monaco and Singapore take place on public roads, which, as they are designed for road cars, are lined with unforgiving barriers. The circuits at Montreal and Melbourne are also street circuits, but both have run-off areas and a more significant number of high-speed corners.

iii. The third type of circuit is the **hybrid**, which consists of tracks with road and street circuit characteristics, such as the one in Abu Dhabi.

13. The Race Weekend

One of the most exciting aspects of F1 is that the drama builds up over the weekend, starting with practice sessions, then qualifying and finally, the race itself.

On race day, which is always on a Sunday, the drivers' positions on the starting grid are determined by the lap times set during the third qualifying round. The driver with the fastest lap time earns pole position, whilst the remaining drivers are ranked in descending order based on their lap times.

Each Grand Prix meeting is held over three days, from Friday to Sunday, except for Monaco, where the first practice sessions are held on a Thursday. Despite this earlier start, the actual race still takes place on Sunday.

Practice Sessions – There are two 90-minute practice sessions on Friday (one in the morning and one in the afternoon) and a 60-minute one on Saturday morning. If a race is scheduled at night, the timings of the practice sessions may vary. Practice sessions allow teams and drivers to familiarise themselves with the track and fine-tune their cars. During practice sessions, the drivers will try different tyres to determine how long they last. They will also closely monitor their fuel consumption (with different tyres) and tune their engines accordingly. They will use this knowledge to help them aim for a good position in the subsequent qualifying rounds.

Qualifying Sessions - These are often the most exciting experiences of a racing weekend and are generally held on Saturday afternoons. The qualifying session aims to determine the drivers' starting positions for the race, ranked from P1, the fastest car (Pole position), down to P20, the slowest car.

The qualifying session is two hours long in its entirety and is split into three sessions:

Q1: This is the first session in which all 20 cars and drivers participate. Each driver will do a set of 'runs', which usually comprise three laps – an 'out' lap, a 'hot' lap and an 'in' lap. They will then return to the pits, change tyres and repeat the process depending on how they performed and how much time is left in the session. At the end of the session, the slowest five cars drop out, forming places 16-20 on the final grid. Q1 lasts for 18 minutes.

Q2: This is the second qualifying session and runs for 15 minutes. It follows the same format as Q1, except that there are only 15 cars and drivers on the circuit. At the end of the 15 minutes, the slowest five are again eliminated, filling the grid spots from 16 to 20.

F1 cars 'spark' because their floor (underside) is only a few millimetres off the ground. F1 cars use titanium skid blocks underneath the chassis which, combined with the undulation of the track, generates the sparks that fly from the beneath the cars as they travel at high-speed. When this happens, it looks pretty spectacular and the car is said to be 'bottoming out'.

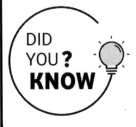

DID YOU **?** **KNOW**

66

Q3: This features the remaining ten cars and lasts for 12 minutes with the drivers competing for pole position. In this session, drivers work really hard to achieve first place on the grid as it gives them a distinct advantage. From a standing start, they are placed a few metres in front of their nearest rival so they stand the best chance of running in first place straight away.

14. The Race

On race day, the drivers and their cars come out onto the track about an hour before the start of the race. They drive one lap and then form the grid based on the order achieved in qualifying. During this time, teams are allowed to make various checks on the cars, such as tyre temperature and pressure, and the drivers can take time to mentally prepare for the race and gain any last-minute advice from their engineers. On the grid (the starting point of the race), they will also undertake any pre-race media duties, such as TV interviews. The cars will set off on a formation lap once the clock ticks around to the race start time. This is one lap of the circuit designed to allow the drivers to make any final adjustments to their car before the race-proper starts. Once they have completed the formation lap, the drivers line their cars up on the grid in qualifying order and wait anxiously for a few seconds until the red lights go out. As soon as they do, the race starts, and now it's all about getting away as fast and as safely as they can. Places can be won or lost at the start, depending on how well the driver performs at this crucial stage.

Those with sharp eyes may notice planks of wood on the floor of F1 cars (although the underside is rarely visible). This is there to ensure that all cars follow the height regulations. At the end of the race, the wear on this block is measured, and if it has worn away by more than 1mm, the car will be disqualified from the race, regardless of where it finished. To prevent this from happening to the cars, the teams place pieces of titanium on parts of the floor to prevent the wooden blocks from wearing out.

The start of the race

There are two different ways to start the race: standing and rolling. If possible, races begin with standing starts, where all the cars are lined up in the position decided by qualifying. However, if the course is exceptionally wet, cars will line up and drive behind a safety car until conditions are deemed safe. The safety car will leave the track, and the race then begins.

For a standing start, the cars will be in their grid position; five red lights appear on the starting board, and then, when these lights go out, the drivers can go. The first corner is always a nervous time for the drivers, team bosses, and those of us watching. After a frantic few opening laps, the race will settle a little, and drivers will continue to lap the circuit until they reach the chequered flag.

How long is an F1 race?

Races last a maximum of two hours and will end in that time window, even if the pre-determined number of laps still needs to be completed. Each race track has a pre-determined number of laps, which varies from race to race, depending on the length of each track. However, if inclement weather conditions halt a race or a nasty crash leads to a red flag, the race can last up to three hours.

Every race on the F1 calendar is designed to last approximately 90 minutes. The minimum distance a Grand Prix can be held over is 305 km miles (190 miles), the only exception being Monaco, which is 260 km (160 miles). The traditional formula for calculating the number of laps is 305 (the minimum distance of a Grand Prix in kilometres) divided by the length of one lap (in kilometres). For example, the track at Spa in Belgium is 7km long, so 350 divided by 7 leaves us with 43.5 laps rounded up to 44 laps.

Race Maximum Time

During a Formula 1 race, the maximum permissible duration for drivers to be in the cars and driving varies from 1 hour and 20 minutes to 1 hour and 40 minutes. The race cannot exceed this time limit due to the cars having limited fuel capacity and refuelling not being permitted during the race. This restriction also ensures that the driver's safety is not compromised, especially on circuits where it is traditionally hot. Also, the drivers need to hydrate and eat after such intense exercise, so being trapped in a cockpit for an extended period is undesirable.

Once the allotted time has passed, an official signals that the drivers have completed the race by waving a chequered flag in front of each driver when they cross the finish line.

15. The Sprint Weekend

On some race weekends, a Sprint Race is added to the schedule. This was introduced as a new format in 2021 with the aim of increasing the excitement for fans and adding a level of unpredictability for the teams. This means that even though a Grand Prix still runs over the course of a weekend, the format of what is known as a 'Sprint Weekend' differs from a normal Grand Prix weekend.

How it works (from 2024 onwards):

A 'sprint shoot-out' takes place on Friday after Free Practice 1. This consists of three qualifying sessions (known as SQ1, SQ2, and SQ3). Every driver enters SQ1; the slowest five are then eliminated at the end of the session. The remaining fifteen drivers enter SQ2, and again, the slowest five are eliminated, leaving ten drivers taking part in SQ3. This session determines the grid for the SPRINT RACE ONLY. The Sprint Race is then run over 19 laps on Saturday morning. The grid lines up according to the results from Sprint Qualifying. A formation lap is run, and then the cars line up for a standing start in exactly the same way as the main race. Due to its length, there are no pit stops in a Sprint Race. All other race rules apply in the same way as for a main Grand Prix. Points are awarded to the first eight finishers.

On Saturday afternoon, the drivers then take part in qualifying for the main race. These sessions are known as Q1, Q2, and Q3 and work on the same basis as sprint qualifying. The slowest five are eliminated from each of Q1 and Q2, leaving ten drivers to fight it out for pole position in Q3.

The results from Q1, Q2 and Q3 dictate the grid positions for the MAIN RACE ONLY, which is run on Sunday.

Whether or not to retain Sprint Weekends as part of the F1 calendar is still under discussion. Whilst they are undoubtedly a lot more entertaining for fans, the pressure on a driver is much greater, as is the stress on the teams.

As of 2024, six venues will host Sprint Races.

16. Key decisions and Strategies

Although many fans adore a good overtake, the critical moments of a race are often determined by the team's strategists on the pit wall rather than the driver in the cockpit. Support team staff will research the best way to run each race and thus create a 'race strategy'.

Why does an F1 team need a strategy?

Drivers must make at least one pit stop during a race unless it's wet throughout. This rule prevents cars from driving in a procession and adds excitement to the race. Refuelling was banned in 2010 (for safety reasons), but to force teams to make pit stop decisions, the FIA mandated that drivers use two types of tyres during any one race. Tyre degradation is critical to the agreed race strategy, and often, teams will have more than one strategy in mind to allow for unforeseen situations.

What influences a team's strategy?

The strategy for a race is determined through extensive research and data analysis, both before and during the race weekend. Before the race, strategists gather data on variables, such as pit stop times, expected time spent in the pit, and likelihood and impact of a safety car. This data, combined with assumptions about the team's and rivals' pace and car performance, is used to develop the basic strategy for the race. During practice and qualifying sessions, teams collect live information on tyre performance from their team and their rivals, which is then used to refine the strategy.

The tyre compound, its temperature, and the car's weight influence the wear of tyres. As fuel is burned off during a race, the car becomes lighter, thus decreasing the impact of wear and tear on the tyres. All this must also be factored in. The teams also need accurate weather predictions, including the chances of rain. Teams must also consider temperature changes to the track and air before and during the race. Wind speed and direction also need to be considered. Teams, therefore, may choose to employ their own meteorologists.

How do teams decide what strategy to use?

A computer processes all the relevant data and calculates the estimated time for a driver to complete a certain number of laps. This calculation considers factors such as traffic and potential delays caused by other vehicles. The aim is to determine the optimal time for the driver to make a pit stop to avoid being held up for too long while maintaining a healthy lead over competitors. The simulation generates the best possible Plan A strategy, including the ideal lap for the driver to make a pit stop and the required lap times. Teams also have a backup Plan B if the first strategy does not work out as expected.

Changes can occur due to various factors, including the car, driver, and other teams. Even weather predictions may not always be accurate. Teams may strategise around the weather by postponing a pit stop in anticipation of rain, which could lead to multiple pit stops. Additionally, teams may respond to a safety car, which reduces the speed of the cars and provides an opportunity for pit stops, resulting in minimal time loss.

Monitoring gaps and changes and adapting to overtake or avoid cars is crucial for strategy. This is where undercuts and overcuts come in.

What are **undercuts** and **overcuts**, and how do they work?

Teams often keep their strategy secret until the last possible moment. However, when a rival pits, teams must decide whether to react or stick to their original plan. The team may take the 'undercut' approach if their driver is stuck behind a competitor. This means the driver pits earlier than planned or earlier than their rival, then sets a few faster laps on new tyres to gain an advantage over their competitor. It is crucial to return to the track in clean air (meaning with no driver immediately in front). Conversely, if a rival pits and the tyres still have plenty of life in them, the team may choose the 'overcut' approach. In this case, the driver stays out longer than planned OR longer than their rival and pushes hard for a few laps, hoping to come out ahead of their competitor after they themselves pit.

Despite all this insight and planning, if a driver makes a mistake, a mechanic fumbles a wheel nut, or if it starts raining unexpectedly, the race can be turned on its head in a moment. When an issue arises, the simulation computers react and assist teams in adapting their strategy.

17. Drag Reduction System (DRS)

Introduced in 2011, the Drag Reduction System (DRS) has significantly enhanced the excitement of F1 races. This contentious device, controlled by the driver via a button on the steering wheel, is designed to facilitate overtaking. When a car is within one second of the one in front, the DRS allows drivers to increase their speed on a straight part of the circuit by opening a slot that eliminates rear-wing drag. This causes the rear wing surface area to decrease, reducing aerodynamic drag and enabling a rapid increase in straight-line speed.

DRS is a complex solution for drivers looking to overtake the car in front. It can only be utilised in specific sections of the track known as DRS activation zones. Although there have been situations where the DRS has been deemed too powerful, allowing drivers to overtake before braking for a turn, its primary purpose is to assist overtaking in situations where drivers would otherwise be stuck in turbulent air. When a car is less than one second behind the car ahead, a signal is sent to the driver behind (via a light on the dashboard), allowing its DRS to be activated. DRS cannot be used for the first lap of a race (new rules for 2024–previously, DRS couldn't be used for the first two laps) after standing or rolling restarts resulting from safety cars or during red flag periods. Additionally, if the FIA race director determines that the conditions are unsafe, they have the authority to deactivate DRS. When several cars are close together, the benefit of using DRS is reduced because the speed boost won't have as much impact.

How many DRS zones are there?

The number of DRS zones varies depending on the characteristics of each track. Typically, each main straight at every track will feature a DRS zone. However, if a circuit has a poor reputation for passing, additional zones may be created, including runs with shallow corners. This is seen in the Baku and Miami courses, where lengthy, meandering zones through the final corners have been added.

If a car's rear wings get stuck open, indicating a system malfunction, drivers will be shown a black flag with an orange disc. In such cases, the driver must return to the pits to allow mechanics to shut the flap manually. If the flap cannot be repaired, it cannot be used again.

IMPORTANT NOTE:

From the beginning of the 2026 season, DRS will be replaced by MOM which stands for Manual Override Mode. The idea is to retain the DRS software and flaps, but for the use of these to change so that drivers can gain an additional energy boost when they need to pass other cars and competitors. Drivers will be able to manually operate this mode.

18. The Safety Car

If there is a crash during a race, the organisers will introduce a safety car to control the speed of the other cars. This allows crashed cars or debris to be safely removed. As a result, all of the other cars will bunch up behind the safety car, and they are not allowed to overtake it until indicated. (This rule is what led to the controversial ending of the 2021 season[1] which I have covered in more detail in section 24). However, some drivers may take advantage of this situation by deciding to pit, which can result in less time lost compared to pitting during the main race.

(AI representation)

Race organisers can also opt to use a *virtual safety car* instead of a physical one. When the *virtual safety car* is used, the FIA will determine an appropriate lap time (like a speed limit) which drivers must stick to. This enables the field to be slowed and gaps between cars maintained, which means those further behind in the race do not gain the advantage they would when bunching up behind a physical safety car. Driving behind the safety car at its slow pace, allows all cars catch up with the front of the pack (even if a driver is a lap down because they are able to unlap themselves during the safety car period) so when the race re-starts, any advantage (in terms of time and gap between their nearest competitor) for those at the front of the race, can be neutralised. Of course, there are strict rules surrounding which type of safety car to use depending on the circumstances and, if the accident or track issue is severe, the race may also be 'red flagged' (stopped entirely) until the track is cleared and deemed safe for the race to resume.

---

1 https://bit.ly/3WElN4m

The safety car may be used during the formation lap in wet weather conditions, as seen in the controversial 2021 Belgian Grand Prix[1]. To signal this, orange lights are illuminated on the start gantry 10 minutes before the race start time, and drivers must fit full-wet tyres in these instances.

19. Communication

<u>How do F1 drivers talk to their team?</u>

Radio communication plays a crucial role in Formula 1 races. The drivers are equipped with a button on their steering wheel that enables them to activate their radio. A microphone and earpiece installed in their helmets help them communicate with their team. Moreover, every driver has a specific engineer assigned to them, who serves as their primary contact during races.

DID YOU? KNOW

The fastest pit stop in F1 history was set by Red Bull and their driver, Max Verstappen during the Brazilian Grand Prix in 2019. The time taken for the pit crew to work on the car and send it back out onto the race track was an incredible **1.82 seconds**! This is less time than it takes to blink five times.

20. The Pit Lane and Pit Stops

Pit stops are essential for cars to change tyres, make repairs and adjust the mechanics of the cars. The drivers must make at least one pit stop to change tyres because the rules specify that each car must use two different tyre compounds during a race.

A pit stop needs to be quick to help the team and driver remain competitive during the race. A pit crew can consist of up to 20 people working together to change four wheels, adjust and change parts if needed and even scrub a driver's visor to help him see. Usually, this happens in under three seconds; however, up to 25 seconds can be lost during pit stops due to slowing down before the stop,

1 https://bit.ly/3wsM8YA

adhering to the pit-lane speed limit and the time taken to rejoin the race.

Pits are located at the side of the track and are positioned based on the previous season's constructors' championship standings. Normally, the champions are closest to pit entry, the runner-up is second closest, and so on, although the champion team reserves the right to select which end.

When drivers and their teams are considering whether or not to 'pit', they will consider the following:

- The state of their tyres
- The state of the race
- What their competitors are doing
- The weather conditions
- Whether there are any mechanical concerns about the car

The team leader in the pit usually reminds the driver to make a pit stop one lap before a pre-scheduled stop.

21. Flags Used In Formula 1

At various points around the circuit, you may see a variety of colourful flags being shown to the drivers. They communicate vital messages to the drivers as they race around the track.

Some of the flags you'll see are:

- **Chequered flag** - At the end of a race, it is shown to the winner and every car that crosses the finish line.
- **Yellow flag** – Indicates danger ahead and warns drivers to slow down.

- **Green flag** – Tells the driver that he has passed a potential danger and normal race conditions now apply.

- **Red flag** – The session (practice, qualifying or the actual race) has been stopped, usually due to an accident, poor track conditions or poor visibility. If this happens on the final lap, the race automatically ends with the drivers 'finishing' in their current positions.

- **Black flag** – Shown when a driver is disqualified from a race.

- **Blue flag** – Warns a driver that he is about to be lapped and to let the faster driver overtake.

During a Grand Prix, if a red flag is shown, the pit lane is closed. All the cars return to the pits and line up in single file at the exit behind the Safety Car. When the cars restart the race, they are arranged in the order they were in when the red flag was shown.

The last time a Black Flag was waved was in 2007 during the Canadian Grand Prix. Two drivers, Felipe Massa and Giancarlo Fisichella, were shown a black flag and disqualified from the race for leaving the pit lane when the red light was still on, i.e., it wasn't safe to do so.

22. Sponsorship

It costs F1 teams exorbitant amounts of money to participate. They must build a competitive car, pay hundreds of staff, and hire expensive drivers to be successful. Sponsorships are essential in F1, and teams have to provide enough value to justify the payment to the sponsor. There are different levels of Formula 1 sponsorship, with the title sponsor being the biggest and paying the most. In return, they get the most benefits and the largest branding space on the car.

Official partners for Formula 1 can pay between $15 million to $50 million per year. The sport wouldn't be able to generate any revenue without the consumerism of fans and the economic interests of businesses.

Who are F1s biggest sponsors?

- Oracle
- Heineken
- Rolex
- INEOS
- Saudi Aramco

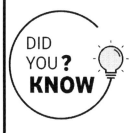

The cost of sponsoring an F1 car depends on where the sponsor would like their name displayed. The most expensive places to sponsor are the large side-pod areas and the rear wing which are the easiest to see when the cars are in full race mode.

At the start of 2022, Red Bull reportedly secured a sponsorship deal with Oracle, a tech giant worth $500 million over five years. This is the largest sponsorship deal in the sport's history. This deal, if true, will bring Red Bull **closer to their budget cap of $135 million** per year (for 2024). They will only need $35 million from their other sponsors to start making a profit, excluding driver salaries and other expenses. Red Bull currently generates more than $40 million each season through their existing sponsors, but this new deal significantly boosts their budget. **The Oracle partnership will provide Red Bull** with financial security, ensuring they remain competitive on the grid for the foreseeable future.

Do F1 drivers have their own sponsors?

Yes. For example, Lewis Hamilton is sponsored by Bose, Tommy Hilfiger and Sony, amongst others. Max Verstappen is sponsored by TAG Heuer.

23. The 1976 Season– Hunt v Lauda

Niki Lauda won the World Championship in 1975 in a Ferrari and continued his winning form in the early races of 1976. By the middle of the season, he seemed sure to win the Championship again until he crashed badly on the second lap of the German Grand Prix at the Nürburgring, and his car burst into flames. Severely injured and badly burned, he was given his last rites in hospital, but Lauda staged a miraculous recovery and, although badly scarred, was racing again just five weeks later at the Italian Grand Prix.

It had already been an acrimonious season of disqualifications and appeals by the time of the accident, with James Hunt a constant thorn in Ferrari's side. In Spain, Hunt controversially ended a run of five Ferrari victories when his McLaren was disqualified initially on a technicality but later reinstated. Then, when he won in Britain, race officials ruled that he should not have participated in the restarted race after his car had been damaged in a multiple first-corner accident.

With just one World Championship race to go, Hunt had closed the gap to within three points. The last race was in Japan, and in appallingly wet and dangerous conditions, Lauda withdrew, believing his life to be more important than another championship win. Even then, Hunt appeared to have lost the title in the confusing final laps, only to learn that he had finished third—just enough to become the 1976 World Champion.

All in all, it had been a remarkable season. Hunt was fortunate to be racing for McLaren because Emerson Fittipaldi was their first choice. Fittipaldi, though, had decided to race for his family's team instead, a decision that prematurely ended his career as a top F1 driver.

24. The 2021 Final Race Controversy

A bit like the 1976 season, the 2021 Championship had many contentious incidents. So, perhaps, it was not surprising that there was controversy on the very last lap of the very last race. The two contenders for the World Championship had exactly the same number of points going into the final race in Abu Dhabi.

Max Verstappen secured pole position in a Red Bull car, but Lewis Hamilton in a Mercedes overtook the Dutchman on the first lap. It looked as though Hamilton had done enough to win when he opened up a lead of over ten seconds (which is a lot in F1), and he was cruising to victory before the mayhem of the final lap.

With four laps of the race remaining, Williams driver Nicholas Latifi crashed into the barriers, resulting in a safety car being called out. While the Mercedes team (of Hamilton) decided they couldn't afford to call Hamilton into the pits in case he lost his lead, Red Bull chose to pit Verstappen and his car was fitted with a new set of soft (faster) tyres. When Verstappen re-entered the track, **five lapped cars** were between him and Hamilton.

The F1 rules state that lapped cars must allow others to pass them in normal racing conditions with overtaking forbidden when there is a safety car on the track. The only way for the lapped cars to be passed by those behind who are faster (in this case, Max Verstappen) is for the safety car to stay out one lap longer than planned and allow the lapped cars to overtake the safety car, complete another lap and rejoin the field at the back in their rightful places.

With only three laps to go and with the safety car still on the track, there were five cars for Max Verstappen to negotiate before he could reach Lewis Hamilton. Max would either have to overtake them in real race time which would be unlikely given there were only a couple of laps remaining, or the safety car could allow those cars through - though this would mean the safety car staying out for one lap longer and the race finishing behind the safety car. Given that this was the last race of the season and the Championship decider, no one wanted to see the race end this way. In order, therefore, for Max and Lewis to race to the flag, the race needed to be restarted (which it was) with at least one lap to go, and Max would need to negotiate the back markers. Though it is likely he would have passed these relatively easily, it would have been difficult for him to get through them and on par with Lewis Hamilton in the short space of one lap. Lewis would therefore have won his eighth World Championship Title.

Then came a flurry of radio calls between the teams in the pits and race director Michael Masi. Initially Masi (who has since left the sport) stated that the lapped cars between Verstappen and Hamilton could not be overtaken whilst behind the safety car. This meets the F1 rules as stated above and meant that the safety car would peel off the track with one lap of the race remaining. Max would then need to pass all five cars plus Lewis Hamilton in that one final lap, to win the race.

(AI representation)

Moments later, however, Masi appeared to change his mind following communication with Red Bull, and ordered the five cars between Max and Lewis to pass the safety car. Crucially, though, he did not allow the lapped cars **behind Max** to overtake.

According to the F1 rules, ALL lapped cars should be allowed to overtake the safety car, not just a few, however if they had all been permitted to overtake, the race would have finished behind the safety car due to the length of time it would take for all runners to pass the safety car and be clear of the front runners for the race to continue safely. By Masi allowing only those cars in-between the two title contenders to pass, he put Max directly behind Lewis on fresh tyres and then brought the safety car into this pits with one lap remaining.

Max therefore had one lap to pass Lewis which he did with ease (due to having new tyres). The idea for Masi doing it this way and not following the rules to the letter, was so that there could be a race to the flag for spectators, however Lewis was effectively a sitting duck and stood no chance of retaining the lead or winning the title. If the rules had been followed, Lewis Hamilton would have won the race and title. Verstappen's win prevented Hamilton from surpassing the record (of most World Championship wins - seven) that he still shares with racing legend Michael Schumacher.

Sportingly, Hamilton congratulated Verstappen, however, Mercedes team principal Toto Wolff was visibly furious. Despite an appeal by the Mercedes team and the opinions of most commentators, the result was (controversially) allowed to stand.

25. Recent Changes

The governing body continually updates the rules to make the sport safer and more exciting. This section may well be out of date by the time you're reading it; nonetheless it's a helpful summary of the types of changes commonly made.

Halo

Since 2018, F1 cars have had to include the halo system in the driver's cockpit. It's a titanium structure designed to protect the driver from flying objects and keep them safer if they crash. It is so strong that it could take the weight of a double-decker bus without breaking.

Grid Kids

Formula 1 has replaced 'grid girls' with 'grid kids'. Formerly, female promotional models appeared on the track before races. They wore clothes with the names of sponsors and held up driver name boards. However, national motorsport authorities now choose children who compete in karting or junior racing categories to perform these duties.

Revised mirrors to improve driver visibility

To enhance driver visibility, the reflective surface of rear-view mirrors on F1's 2023 cars was widened from 150mm to 200mm. After Red Bull and Mercedes conducted tests in Hungary and Belgium in 2022, the entire grid increased their rear-view mirror sizes for the Dutch Grand Prix, leading to their adoption.

26. Superstitions

Due to the dangerous nature of their jobs and desire for success, many drivers turn to superstitious behaviours, rituals and good luck charms.

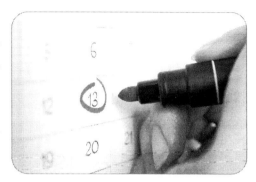

a) Stefano Modena was not fond of the left-hand side of the garage.

Stefano Modena, an Italian Formula One driver who drove in 70 Grand Prix races during the late 1980s and early 1990s, was known for his peculiar habits. While some of them, such as his preference for fastening his belts in a certain way and always entering the car from the left, were harmless, others affected those around him. In Martin Brundle's book 'Working the Wheel' the former Brabham teammate shared one of Modena's eccentric moments after pre-qualifying for the Brazilian Grand Prix in 1989.

"We had an hour to move the cars and all our equipment into a proper garage, one that was being vacated by a team that had failed to pre-qualify. Sweat was pouring off the mechanics as they humped all the toolboxes and air cylinders, and other heavy pieces into the garage and tried to get the cars ready for the start of the official practice."

"They had just about completed the job when my teammate Stefano Modena walked in and looked like he had seen a ghost. 'No! No!' he said. 'I don't want my car on the left; it must be on the right.' Stefano was a lovely guy, but he was very, very superstitious. He would not get into his car if it was on the left-hand side of the garage. There was nothing for it but to move the cars and equipment around."

"I am still very superstitious and always was," Modena told Motor Sport Magazine in 2014. "I didn't care about being different; this was my character, and it was my results that mattered, not how much I smiled or my superstitions."

So, what about wearing his gloves inside out? "This was not superstition - it was because the seams on the inside were cutting my fingers, making my skin very sore."

Well, that clears that up, then.

b) Alan Jones won the 1980 world driver's title in Canada after receiving a last-minute delivery of his lucky charm: a pair of red underpants.

"I'm superstitious, and I felt uneasy because I thought I'd lost them," admitted the Australian after the race. "But Bev (his wife) drove to Brands Hatch in England, where I'd left them in a motorhome and rushed them here (to Montreal) by special delivery."

c) Another driver, David Coulthard, also had an underwear superstition.

It may seem strange, but Jones is not the only Formula 1 driver with a habit of always wearing the same underwear while racing. In his younger years, David Coulthard found success while wearing a pair gifted to him by his aunt. When he reached Formula 1, the undergarments were no longer wearable, but Coulthard kept them with him at every Grand Prix for good luck.

"Then one day a McLaren employee was cleaning my things, saw these pants - which in all fairness were by then over a decade old and threw them away," Coulthard recounted wistfully in his autobiography.

d) Felipe Massa is another driver who has admitted to occasionally getting too attached to his underwear.

"Sometimes when I start the weekend, on Saturday, for example, and things are going well, I keep the same underwear," he said. "We (drivers) are a little bit crazy sometimes– it doesn't change anything by using this underwear or another one, but it just makes you feel relaxed; you have everything you had yesterday, and yesterday was a good day. When it's not a good day, you change everything!"

27. Formula One Terminology

Now that you understand what F1 is all about, let's examine some of the slang used. The words listed below are some of the technical jargon used by the teams, staff, and commentators. Once you know them, you will be in a better position to understand what some 'expert commentators' are talking about when they use terms such as 'marbles' and 'porpoising'.

Blistering/Graining - Blistering occurs when a track's cold surface causes the warmer inside of the tyre to blow out, resulting in pieces of the tyre being expelled. On the other hand, graining happens when the tyres are cold, and the hotter outside surface causes rubber chunks to detach and cling to the tyre.

Box - As a helpful aid to drivers during a race, the term 'box' reminds pit controllers that a pit stop is imminent or scheduled for the next lap. The word 'box' is derived from the German term 'boxenstopp,' which translates to 'pit stop.'

Brake Bias - Allows the drivers to adjust the difference between how much the front and the rear wheels brake. Usually, when a driver pushes the brake pedal, the front and rear wheels break evenly. In wet conditions, the driver may want to use the rear brakes more than those at the front of the car. Drivers adjust brake biases throughout a race to balance the car depending on the condition of the tyres, the course and the amount of fuel left in the tanks.

Degradation - When the tyres lose grip (due to wear) they are said to 'degrade'. This negatively affects the tyre performance and pace and is often referred to simply as 'deg' or 'tyre deg'.

Dirty Air/Clean Air - Dirty air is the turbulent air left in the wake of a car. The car coming in behind will experience a drag because of this dirty air. Clean air is what drivers experience when there is no car immediately in front of them.

Marbles - Tiny pieces of rubber that are shredded from the tyres while cornering are called marbles. They accumulate off the racing line, and driving on them can be dangerous as the car can lose traction.

Porpoising - When the car bounces on its suspension. This issue can be caused by a combination of suspension and aerodynamics or simply by a bumpy track. Running a car closer to the ground or setting up a stiffer ride can lead to porpoising, which creates two sorts of problems. First, it hampers the car's performance and reliability. Second, it can create a major health concern for the drivers.

Fun F1 Driver Facts:

- James Hunt played at Junior Wimbledon
- Kimi Raikkonen was an Army Corporal and a mechanic – all Finnish males aged 18 have to undertake 12 months of military service.
- Charles Leclerc is a very competent piano player.
- Lewis Hamilton is a competent guitar player and pianist. There is footage on social media of him playing *Imagine* (by John Lennon) and the Adele song *Someone Like You.*

Chapter Three

FOOTBALL

"Some people think football is a matter of life and death. I don't like that attitude. I can assure them it is much more serious than that."

Bill Shankly

CONTENTS

1. What is Football?

In a nutshell, football is a game played by two teams of eleven players who aim to score a goal against their opponents by kicking a football into the opposition's net. Players must use their feet or heads to score these goals, and individuals are penalised if they use their hands or arms to assist. The team that scores the most goals by the end of the game is declared the winner.

FAMOUS ENGLISH FOOTBALL PLAYERS.—1881.

Football is the world's most popular ball game in terms of the number of participants and spectators. Few other sports experience the level of passion from players and fans alike, which is a trademark of the game.

In some parts of the world, football is also known as soccer, and regardless of where you encounter it, the game has a rich history. The modern version—which we are familiar with now—originated in England during the mid-19th century; however, earlier variations of the game are also considered to be part of its history.

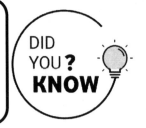

The weight of a football is between 410 and 450 grams, which is about the weight of a loaf of bread or four bananas!

DID YOU? KNOW

Football is also affectionately called 'chess on a green pitch' in reference to the moving and placing of players in a tactical way to secure victory. In the United States and Canada, English football is always known as 'soccer' to differentiate it from the American national game of football – American Football. This game differs from English football in many ways, primarily with its use of an oval ball instead of a round one and allowing players to pass the ball with their hands. American Football is perhaps closer in style to rugby.

2. Equipment

- A football – a round leather ball with a circumference of 68-70 cm
- Two goals
- Two nets
- Football boots and football clothing (known as 'kit')

Every player must wear appropriate equipment for the game. Their clothing must include a jersey, footwear (football boots), shorts, and stockings with shin pads. Incidentally, goalkeepers must wear different colours (jerseys and shorts) from their teammates to allow referees to distinguish them from the other players more easily. If an outfield player takes over the goalkeeper role, they must change their kit accordingly.

3. Development (History)

As briefly mentioned, the game of football has ancient origins, and there is evidence of its existence in various cultures and regions more than two to three thousand years ago. The Aztecs (the dominant occupiers of Mexico before the Spanish conquest in the 16th Century) played a game called 'tlachtli' using a bouncing rubber ball, and players were not allowed to use their hands. Similarly, an exercise known as Tsu' Chu was popular in ancient China which involved using a leather ball filled with feathers and hair, along with a small net. Though we know that the modern form of the game originated in England during the mid-19th century (see section 1. What is Football?), it is worth also noting that this is the time when Rugby Football and Association Football became separate sports, which is when we saw the creation of the Football Association (FA).

Going back further, before the advent of the current game, there is a long-standing belief that football's origins date back to 12th century England. Records show that games resembling football were being played in meadows and on roads, and, at this time, the players would not only kick the ball, but they would also punch it with their fists. Undoubtedly, this version of football was considerably rougher than today's, however, some players still exhibit questionable behaviour, which may indicate that there has not been as much progress as initially believed.

Each team consists of eleven players, but early versions were played by large numbers of people and covered more extensive areas of land. This meant there was a lack of structure, which sadly led to several injuries and even deaths, resulting in the game (in that form) being banned. Despite the ban, football remained popular and was seen on the streets of London once more in the 17th century.

Schools at the time continued to play a variation of football and were able to maintain a more structured approach. Two prominent schools, Rugby and Eton, created different versions of the game; in Rugby, players were allowed to use their hands, while at Eton, they were only permitted to use their feet. This version from Eton went on to become the foundation of the game we play today.

Rules were still not standardised, though, so efforts were made in both 1848 and 1863 to do this. The latter date is the year in which the Football Association was established in London. The main standardisations related to the prohibition of the use of hands to carry the ball and the size and weight of the ball, which were to be the same in every game. With the differences between the two games (those played at Rugby and Eton) now being formalised, it was decided that the game should be separated into two codes: Football and Rugby. The rules still remained relatively flexible, though, with teams being allowed to wear any shirts they preferred and with differing numbers of players on the field.

Following industrialisation, larger groups began meeting at places like factories, pubs and churches. This led to the facilitation and formation of football teams in larger cities. Surprisingly, football clubs have existed since the 15th century, but they were disorganised and did not have any form of official status.

The oldest (current) football club is Notts County, which was formed in 1862.

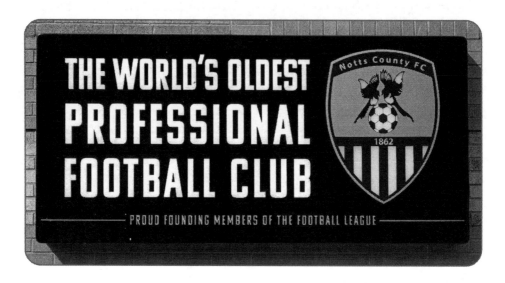

Initially, public school teams dominated the game, but later, teams consisting of workers became the common majority. Clubs then started paying players to join their teams, which eventually led to the development of football as a (paid) professional sport. Fan interest was also increasing, and football started to become popular with members of the 'working class'. Large crowds of up to 30,000 were noted at some matches in the late 19th century.

In 1885, Professional Football was established, which was a huge step forward. Before then, the game had been played by 'amateurs' (i.e. those not being paid), and when clubs started paying to encourage the best players into their teams, it caused many issues between rival clubs. Some clubs would create 'jobs' with different titles to hide the fact that they were paying players to play football, so it was a relief when clubs could legally pay players with the legalisation of Professional Football in 1885. Three years later, in 1888, the Football League was established. Initially, it comprised of only twelve clubs in its first season, but these numbers grew as more clubs joined, leading to multiple divisions of the league being created. In 1908, football was accepted as an Olympic sport, with teams taking part in the games of that year, and then in 1930, the FIFA (Fédération Internationale de Football Association – the sport's governing body) World Cup was created. This is now considered to be the most prestigious national-level tournament.

4. The Objective

The objective of football is to score the most goals (balls in the net) whilst defending your own goal (net) from the opposition. A player can pass the ball to anyone else on the field and, unlike some sports, can run with the ball at their feet (called dribbling) but cannot (as previously mentioned) use their hands. When it comes to passing the ball, there are a few rules players need to abide by:

- The first is the offside rule, which we'll come to later.
- The second relates to passing the ball back to their own goalkeeper. If a player passes the ball back to the keeper using their feet, the goalkeeper must play the ball with their feet, too. If the ball is headed back, then the keeper is allowed to pick up the ball.

5. The Game Itself

A football match lasts ninety minutes and is divided into two halves of forty-five minutes. An interval – known as half time - between the two sessions is usually fifteen minutes. After each forty-five-minute playing time has elapsed, the referee can decide if additional playing time should be added. This can be if, for example, a player has been injured and the game has been paused whilst they were being attended to. Just before the end of each half, you will see a Match Official standing on the touchline (line around the playing pitch), holding up a board to indicate how many additional minutes will be added.

The basics

- Before the match begins, the referee tosses a coin that decides which team 'kicks off' (kicks the ball first) and at which end each team will begin the match.
- The ball is then kicked from the centre spot, up and down the field between players, until a goal is scored. The rules have been recently changed to allow the kick-off to be passed back as well as forwards if preferred. Previously it was only possible to kick the ball forwards.
- The ball is returned to the centre spot at the start of each half (and after a goal is scored).
- No players are allowed to be in their opposition half (of the pitch) at kick-off.
- Any foul can result in a free kick.

- If the ball is kicked beyond the goal line by the attacking team, the defending team restarts play with a goal kick. If the defending team kicks it behind their own goal line, the attacking team are awarded a corner kick.
- A goal kick must be taken on the edge of the six yard box, but can be taken by either a defender or goalkeeper. A corner kick is taken by the attacking side, where the ball is placed in a corner, where there is a small quarter circle.
- If the ball leaves the field of play on either side of the pitch, the other team has a throw in. The player throwing the ball back into play must hold it in both hands above their head and have both feet on the ground behind the touchline before releasing it from behind their head onto the pitch.
- Tackling is the skill of taking the ball away from an opponent. What's important when you tackle is that you touch the ball with one of your feet. If you make contact with the player rather than the ball, that is a foul, meaning the opposition get to take a free kick.

The following fouls will be **penalised**:

- **Dangerous challenges** - even if a player doesn't make contact with anyone, a referee might award a free kick to the opposition.
- **Handball** – players can touch the ball with their feet, head, chest, thighs and even shoulders, but not with any part of an arm.
- **Diving/Simulation** - if a player pretends to have been fouled, referees are allowed to call a free kick against that player.
- **Being offside** (more later).
- **Foul throw** - when a ball is thrown in from the sideline, it must be kept behind the head before it is thrown.

If these rules are broken, referees are allowed to penalise the culprits. The referee can award a yellow card (for less severe offences) or a red card (for more serious misdemeanour's). If a player is given two yellow cards in a game, they are punished as if they had received a red card. If a player is shown a red card, they are immediately removed from the game and can play no further part.

Should a player be shown a yellow card, they are (unlike in Rugby) allowed to stay on the pitch. However, during tournaments, if a player has received a yellow card earlier in a competition, they will not usually be able to play in the following match. So, the team against which they committed the offence doesn't benefit, but the next opponents will.

The Football Pitch (Dimensions)

A standard football pitch measures approximately 100 metres in length and 60 metres in width, and for official games, there are specific regulations regarding the minimum and maximum dimensions allowed. FIFA, the world governing body for football, sets these standards, and all pitches used for official games must adhere to them:

- Length - minimum of 90 metres (100 yds) and maximum of 120 metres (130 yds)
- Width - minimum 45 metres (50 yds) and maximum of 90 metres (100 yds)

In the 1800s, pitches could be up to 100 yards wide and 200 yards long (91 and 182 metres), so they were substantially bigger. At that time, the boundary lines (around the pitch) were marked by flags until 1882, when permanent lines replaced them. Five years later, a centre circle was added, becoming standard and mandatory.

The pitch below shows most of the key markings and labels associated with the game. The goalmouth is the small box inside the penalty area. The game's laws stipulate that the goalmouth line must be 5.5 metres from the goal line and the penalty area 18 yards (16.4 metres) from the goal line. The penalty box was introduced in 1887 and was later complemented by a D-shaped curve in 1937.

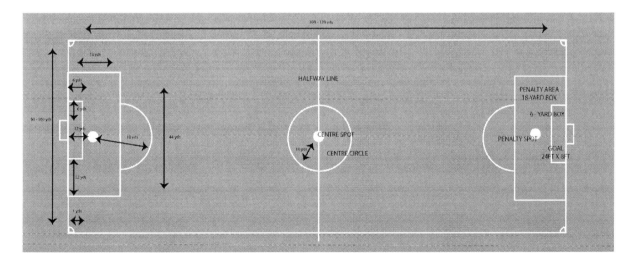

Today, the goal comprises vertical and horizontal posts (the one above the goalie's head is known as the crossbar), but these were not introduced until 1882. It was a further ten years before a net was added.

Starting the Game

To begin a football game, the referee tosses a coin. The captain of the visiting team then chooses heads or tails. The outcome of the toss in football is less crucial than in other sports, though some teams prefer to play the second half with their fans in front of them. The winning captain (of the toss) decides which end of the field their team will start from, and the losing team will kick off the game. For the second half, players change ends, and the team who did not kick off at the beginning will kick off in the second half. Play must not begin until the referee blows the whistle.

Playing Positions

There are four playing positions as follows:

- Goalkeeper - only one
- Defender - usually three or four depending on the chosen strategy
- Mid-fielder - again, usually three or four depending on the strategy
- Striker or Attacker - usually two or three, depending on the strategy

6. Strategies and Play Formations

The core of football tactics is in the formation of the team. It is the manager's job to determine the team's strategy for each game. It is, therefore, their job to also decide on the team's formation. There are many formations currently in use, however the most common ones are:

Classic 4-4-2

This formation is one of the oldest in football. It consists of four defenders, four mid-fielders, and two attackers, and its key is in its partnerships. The two strikers, midfield pairing, full-back, and wingers each need a telepathic understanding of their role on the pitch.

How it works:

The wide mid-fielders use pace to get themselves in position to cross the ball towards the goal and aim at their strikers. Often, these strikers complement each other by having a different set of skills, for example, a tall striker who is good in the air and a smaller, more agile one who can work with any knocked-down balls.

Pros and Cons:

The weakness of the 4-4-2 formation is its rigidity and the amount of work expected of the two central midfield players. In this formation, the central mid-fielders need to be supremely fit and comfortable both attacking and defending. In modern football, it's more fashionable to have at least three players operating in and around the centre of the pitch, adjusting the format to 4-3-3. An excellent example of a team successfully using the 4-4-2 formation is the treble-winning Manchester United side of the late 90s[1].

Tiki-Taka

Anyone who has watched European football over the past ten years will have witnessed the rise of Tiki-Taka football. Barcelona and Spain have adopted it with great results, winning league titles, European Cups and international tournaments. In this form of the game, players make short passes, with the key to success coming from loading the midfield with technically gifted players who can retain possession (of the ball) for significant periods of the game.

Intelligent and agile attacking players are added outside the mid-fielders who can create space for play and drag their opposing player out of position. A popular footballing idiom states that 'if the opposition haven't got the ball, they can't score', and Tiki-Taka adopts this by aiming for ball possession at least 60-70% of the game.

Tiki-Taka football has declined in recent years, primarily as opposition teams have managed to counter-attack and press the team in possession so they don't get anywhere near the goal.

---

1 https://bit.ly/3ylt3YB

Today, the most common response to a Tiki-Taka team is to sit back and allow the opposition to play in front of you, remaining as compact as possible so that you can sniff out any danger in the final third of the pitch. When the ball is lost, teams employing the Tiki-Taka formation can be found lacking numbers in defence, where this system requires players to be more up-field rather than back, defending their own goal.

The Counter-attack

Whilst Tiki-Taka has declined in recent years, its place has been taken by the most devastating tactic– the counter-attack.

How it works:

A team using this method will work to draw their opposition into their defensive third, from where they will then launch a counter-attack. This is done by stealing the ball from the opposition and setting off at breakneck speed. The idea is that once you have taken the ball from your opposition and because you have drawn them down the pitch, they will have left several gaps in their defence, which can be exploited by swift running. Counter-attacking sides are often split into two units—defence and attack. The defensive unit sits deep and tight, pouncing on any loose ball to regain possession, at which point it will pass the ball quickly forward to its attacking unit. These attacking players are often fast and skilful, so they can sprint into gaps and create one-on-one situations with defenders. The key to the counter-attack is getting the ball forward at pace. For it to work, teams need attackers who are better players than their opposition defenders.

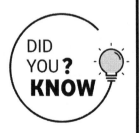

DID YOU **?** **KNOW**

When watching a game on TV, in the top corner (usually), you will see the score. For example, in a game between Germany and France you might see: GER 2 - FRA 3. This means that France are beating Germany by 3 goals to 2 and that Germany (being mentioned first) are playing at home. This does not apply in tournaments like the World Cup. Often the broadcasters will also depict the flag of the two teams beside the score.

Scoring Goals

A goal is defined as when the 'whole' of the ball crosses the goal line, which has, over the years, caused much controversy. In 1986, there was an incident at the World Cup in Mexico when Diego Maradona (an Argentinian player) scored a goal against England in the quarter-final of the Cup. English players on the pitch argued for a foul, stating that Maradona had punched the ball with his hand; however, the referee disagreed, and the goal was allowed. This incident later became known as 'The Hand of God' when television replays showed that Maradona had touched the ball with his hand.

It was, though, too late for the decision to allow the goal to be reversed. Since then, technology has been introduced to help settle many controversial issues in football; for example, there is now a microchip in the ball which helps determine whether a goal has been scored (i.e., if the ball crossed the goal line), where on the pitch a foul was committed and whether or not the ball left the pitch.

7. Video Assisted Referee (VAR)

In 2010, Video Assistant Referees (VAR)s were conceived, and they are now used in most top-level football games. The concept allows specific incidents to be reviewed by the referee or the VAR team during play. The purpose is to improve decision-making, but it is not without controversy. Some argue that decisions should not be 'referred at all', saying that using VAR spoils the flow of the game. They may have a point, as some decisions can take several minutes to be made.

The basics

A team of three individuals reviews the referee's decisions by analysing video footage of the relevant action from various camera angles. Currently, VAR is used to review four types of decisions: goals and any violations that preceded them, red cards given, penalties awarded and cases of mistaken identity during the awarding of yellow or red cards. The VAR team can overturn the referee's decision; however, the error must be 'clear' for this to occur.

The review process

Reviewing a decision typically works in one of two ways: either the VAR team can suggest a review, or the referee can request one after making a decision.

In the first scenario, if the VAR team determines that a clear error has occurred, they must notify the referee. After this, the referee has three options:

1. Immediately overturn the decision based on the VAR's advice
2. Stick with the initial decision
3. Review the incident themselves on a monitor at the side of the pitch

What happens when a decision is being reviewed?

If an incident needs to be reviewed, the VAR team will study the footage and notify the referee through an earpiece of their findings. When this happens, the referee will advise the players that the review findings are ready by pointing to their ear. Any appropriate action will then be taken.

How long does the VAR team have to flag up an incident they spotted?

After an incident and if the VAR team spot something requiring further investigation, they have until the game next restarts to alert the referee. If play is ongoing, the VAR team must wait until the ball goes out of play before notifying the referee to stop the game while they are reviewing. If the team fails to do this in time and the game is restarted, the referee's decision can no longer be overturned. Allowing the referee to review incidents and the VAR team to overturn the initial decision is now an integral part of the game.

8. Playing Styles

The styles of play often depend on which continent the team comes from, with significant differences between Europe, for example, and South America. World Cups are always exciting because it is a time when several different styles can be seen clashing against each other.

Here's a look at six of the most-known football styles from across the world:

British
Players: Physical, Quick, Direct.
Style of Play: The no-nonsense style of British football is the oldest and is still used

in the Premier League. Attacks are typically set up quickly with direct long balls over the defence, usually bypassing the mid-fielders entirely. This fast-paced style leads to 50/50 contests for the ball and can be very exciting, though it can lead to loss of possession, which means it is also a risky style of play.

Italian

Players: Skilful, Crafty, Cautious.

Style of Play: The Italian style is cautious, committing very few players to attack. Forward players often make diagonal, indirect runs, which are difficult for defenders to anticipate and keep in check. Defenders like to slow down the tempo of a game and flood their side of the field with numerous defenders to pressure and slow down opposition attacks.

Latin

Players: Confident with the ball, good dribblers, Innovative

Style of Play: The Latin game differs significantly from the European style. The players are shorter and more robust than their European counterparts, so they aim to keep possession of the ball with free-flowing passes. Like the British game, it has a fast pace, though its structure is minimal. This style of play can lead to defensive weaknesses prone to counter-attacks.

Northern Europe

Players: Aggressive, Fast, Organised

Style of Play: The game is played directly with determined but anticipated attacks. Defensively, a formation is always maintained. Each player has a specific job and rarely improvises. These teams usually keep possession or try to overwhelm the opposition with numbers when attacking. Although this style could be more attractive to watch, it is very effective.

Continental

Players: Good passers, collectivists

Style of Play: Attacks are generated with creativity, but there is still composure and team communication. Players roam freely through different positions to accommodate the style of football, and defensively, they put a lot of pressure on the attacking team to regain possession. This method of play originated in the Netherlands and revolutionised the game of football. Many teams adopted this play style, now known as the Continental style. <u>Central American</u>

Players: Crafty, Excessive Dribblers

Style of Play: The players use short passes and dribble the ball with their feet to move around. Quick runs at the opposition are rare. The tempo and build-up of the game are generally slow, except for the occasional long ball that is sent up to the forwards.

No matter what style is played, one vital skill is the ability to look for and create space. Andrés Iniesta, one of the best players of modern times, was once asked for the secret of his success. He replied, *"Before I receive the ball, I quickly look to see who I can pass it to. I look to see who is around me, and crucially, I try to get into space to receive the next pass. The more space I have, the more time I have to think. I need to consider where my teammate is running to, whether he will be onside, which one has the space, and how they like to receive the ball, to their feet or in front of them."*

This is an excellent illustration of how football, like art, is about appreciating space. The best players do this through hard work and design, not by accident.

9. Decision Making

A football player continuously makes decisions throughout a game. They must decide when and how to perform every action on the pitch, including passing, shooting, finding openings, and choosing an attacker to defend or a defender to attack.

Excellent decision-making on the pitch is just as crucial as developing muscle strength and footwork skills.

Some of the decisions that players must make:

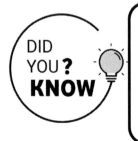

DID YOU **?** **KNOW**

There is an arc painted on the pitch in the penalty area to make sure that all players comply with the ten-yard rule.

- Whether to play a defensive or attacking style
- Whether to pass or shoot
- Whether to steal or guard as a defender
- Whether to dribble or pass the ball
- Which type of shot on goal to make

- Assess where teammates, the ball and opponents are
- Defenders – in particular - need to decide whether to tackle or just shield (prevent) the attacker from reaching the goal (net)
- How to get into a space that allows teammates to pass the ball to you
- To anticipate where the ball may go next, often by focusing on the ball's potential trajectory even before it is played. Watching the body language of other players can help with this particular decision

10. Basic Football Regulations

- All outfield players can only use their feet, chest, or head. The goalkeeper is allowed to use their hands but can only touch the ball inside their own penalty area.

- The one primary purpose of the football offside rule (see section 12) is to ensure that opponents are between the attacking player receiving the ball (looking to score) and the goal. Those opponents include, but are not limited to, the defending goalkeeper and at least one other player. The attacking player in contact with the ball will commit an offside offence if there is no opposing player between them and the goal when they receive the ball.

- A foul is generally the use of excessive force or handling of the ball by an outfield player. As previously discussed, fouls committed during the game usually result in disciplinary action. Following a foul or alleged misconduct, the referee may award a free kick to be taken from where the foul was committed.

- There are two different types of free kick: indirect and direct. When a player takes a direct free kick, they can shoot the ball into the goal from a stationary position. On the other hand, with an indirect free kick, the ball must first come into contact with another player before a shot at the goal can be made.

- Before taking a direct free kick, opposing players often form a wall to protect their goal. They must be a minimum distance of ten yards from the ball. The referee will adjudicate where the foul took place and, for the benefit of all players and spectators, will mark out ten metres away by spraying a line on the pitch from a can. This is a line that defending players may not cross. If the foul was committed inside the penalty area, the referee will award a penalty kick by pointing to the penalty spot.

The offside rule was first introduced by the FA in 1863!

DID YOU? KNOW

11. Penalties

Firstly, the referee must decide whether a player committed a foul. If so, did the foul occur inside or outside the penalty area?

When a foul is committed within the penalty area, the referee, often with the aid of technology, will blow their whistle and award a direct shot at the goal. He will do this by pointing to the penalty spot. The team awarded the penalty will select a player to take the shot.

When a penalty is awarded, the ball is placed on the penalty spot, and the designated player steps up. All players, except for the kicker and the goalkeeper, must exit the penalty area but remain on the field.

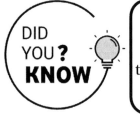

Before taking the kick, the goalkeeper can move around but must remain positioned on the goal line between the posts. The goalkeeper must face the kicker

If the ball hits the referee, the game automatically stops and the ball is dropped between two players, one from each team.

and is prohibited from making contact with the goalposts, crossbar, or net. As soon as the kick is taken, the goalkeeper must have one foot touching or aligning with the goal line.

The referee will indicate that the penalty taker may take the kick by blowing the whistle. During the run-up to the ball, the kicker can pretend to move in either direction, but they cannot do so after completing the run-up. The kick and the last step taken by the kicker must be done in one motion. Once the ball has been kicked, it is considered in play; other players can enter the penalty area. The kicker can only touch the ball again once another player touches it or it goes out of play.

Once the kick is taken, standard rules continue to apply.

12. The Offside Rule

The offside rule was introduced to stop players hanging around their opponent's goal and simply waiting for the ball to be passed to them for scoring.

A player can only be offside in their opponents' half of the pitch. If any part of their body is closer to the opponents' goal line than both the ball and the second last opponent, a player is in an offside position. Being level is not offside. The key is that being in an offside position in itself is not an offence. It only becomes an offence if a player is deemed to be 'affecting play'. 'Affecting play' doesn't only mean 'receiving the ball', it could also be preventing a goalkeeper from diving to save a shot, blocking the goalkeepers' line of sight or just preventing a defender from doing their job.

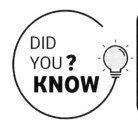

The first FA Cup Final was held at Wembley Stadium in 1923.

Note - players are allowed to stand on the goal line if they want, but the ball cannot come to them without that player being declared as offside.

The offside rule is a fundamental concept but is by no means easy for players, referees and linesmen to judge, so you'll commonly hear commentators discuss offside decisions. There is a common debate about what is considered good for the game versus the strict and literal application of its laws, specifically the offside rule.

13. Kick-off and Re-Starts

The game resumes with a kick-off after the scoring of every goal. All players should be in their team's half before each kick-off. The team which concedes a goal restarts play with a new kick-off.

14. The Domestic Game

The domestic game is far more important to many football fans than international football. This is due (amongst other issues) to the number of games played domestically and the rivalry between the clubs and their fans.

During the early days of professional football, clubs often organised 'friendly' matches between two sides; however, this was an unreliable source of income for many clubs, so William McGregor, director of Aston Villa, proposed the idea of a Football League. On 2nd March 1888, he sent a letter to Blackburn Rovers, Bolton Wanderers, Preston North End, and West Bromwich Albion – many cities with some now-famous clubs (Liverpool, London, Manchester) were not included in this letter. They had no representation amongst the original members of the Football League.

The inaugural meeting of the newly proposed Football League was held on 23rd March 1888, the eve of the FA Cup Final (held between West Bromwich and Preston at the Kennington Oval). Once the teams agreed, the Football League's first season officially kicked off on 8th September 1888, with 12 member clubs.

15. The Football League

The Leagues

English domestic football has four divisions or leagues, with 92 clubs. Until 1992, they were named The First Division, the Second Division, the Third Division and the Fourth Division. Below this, there are non-league Divisions. After 1992, the First Division was renamed the Premiership and consisted of 20 clubs; the Second Division was renamed the Championship and consisted of 24 clubs, with the final two divisions, the Third and Fourth, being renamed League One and League Two.

Promotions, Regulations and Playoffs

Every season, the top three teams in each league move up a league for the next season, while the bottom three teams drop down a league unless they are already in the top or bottom divisions. This applies to various leagues across the country. Sometimes, playoffs determine specific team promotions/demotions (see below).

English Football League Playoffs

At the end of the season, in all leagues, a champion is determined by their playing record over the whole season.

Before 1987, clubs in the bottom three leagues at the end of the season would automatically drop down a league for the following season—known as relegation. In the same way, the top three clubs from the league below moved up to the successive league—known as promotion. The exact number of teams remained the same in each league. In 1987, the authorities introduced a new system to determine which clubs were promoted and relegated to and from the Premiership and the other three leagues. The two highest-ranking clubs from the Championship would continue to be automatically promoted, but the clubs ranked from third to sixth would take part in a mini-tournament to compete for the third promotion spot. This is known as the playoffs.

There are playoffs to determine the third spot in the Championship and Leagues One and Two. The playoffs conclude with a final match held at Wembley Stadium. The one for the clubs trying to get to the Premier League is often referred to as the 'richest game in world football' because the winning team receives a portion of the Premier League TV revenue.

16. Rules or Laws?

In football, rules are known as laws, hence the expression 'according to the laws of the game'. There are 17 laws. I will summarise a few of them below:

i. <u>No hands</u>

Most people, even those who know nothing about football, understand that players are not allowed to use their hands in the game unless they are the goalkeeper; however, it is worth qualifying a couple of points:

- 'Hand' includes any part of the body from fingertips up to, but excluding, the shoulder.
- Players are not allowed to handle the ball intentionally.
- If a ball is kicked and accidentally hits a player's hand or arm, it is not considered a handball. It is up to the referee to use their judgment to determine if the contact was accidental or deliberate.
- Surprisingly, there are also rules regarding goalkeepers and their hands. They can only pick up a ball passed from their teammates if it has been headed to them. If the ball has been kicked to them, they must also kick it. If the goalkeeper breaks this rule, the referee will award an indirect kick from the point of the offence.

ii. <u>Throw-ins</u>

A throw-in is taken when the ball crosses a sideline and leaves the field of play. The two basic football laws for a proper throw-in are to have both feet on the ground and to throw the ball with both hands over the head.

iii. <u>Corner Kicks & Goal Kicks</u>

When the ball goes out of bounds across the goal line, a corner kick or goal kick is taken, depending on which team touched the ball last. If the attacking team touched it last, a goal kick is awarded. However, a corner kick is given if the defending team last touches the ball. Any player can take the goal kick from anywhere inside the penalty area. A corner kick in a football match is taken from the corner nearest to where the ball went out of play.

iv. Fouls

In terms of fouls, a general guideline is that if it appears to be a foul, it is most likely one. Players are prohibited from kicking, tripping, jumping, charging, striking, pushing, holding, or spitting at their opponents. While it should be straightforward to determine if a foul has occurred, football is a physical and contact sport, and there may be situations where players can bump or go shoulder-to-shoulder while competing for the ball. As long as their hands or elbows do not come up, this is not necessarily a foul. As with all fouls, they are judgment calls, and each referee may see these differently.

A summary of some fouls:

- Dangerous challenges - even if a player doesn't make contact with anyone, a referee can still consider a tackle dangerous.
- Handball – players can touch the ball with their feet, head, chest, thighs and even shoulders, but not with any part of an arm.
- Diving/Simulation - if a player pretends to have been fouled, referees are allowed to penalise that player.
- Being Offside – more later
- Foul throw - when a ball is thrown in from the sideline, it must be kept behind the head before being thrown in.

17. Football Fans

Two distinct fan culture traditions exist: the British and the South American.

The British fans adopted the practice of singing songs inspired by the pub and working-class tunes, while South American fans embraced the carnival style, incorporating firecrackers and fireworks. Other countries' fans have since adopted a combination of these traditions.

18. Football Tournaments

a. Domestic Club

The Football Association Challenge Cup (FA Cup) was the first significant football tournament, beginning in 1871. It is more than just a showpiece occasion; it was (until the advent of the Premier League in 1992 the most prestigious (and virtually the only) match on television. All teams could enter, and after the first two rounds, the teams from the top divisions joined in. So, at that stage, it is possible for a team from a low division to be drawn against Manchester United or Liverpool. It is the only way in which a team of postmen, office clerks and production line workers could get the chance to walk out at Old Trafford, Anfield or Stamford Bridge.

b. European Club Tournaments

The most prestigious club tournament in football is the UEFA Champions League, which began in the 1992-1993 season. Before this, the Tournament was known as the European Cup. It has become even more popular by introducing a mini-league group stage system, similar to the World Cup format. The competition has also expanded to include more clubs, increasing from the initial 8 to 32. A club which wins the tournament three times in a row can keep the Champions League trophy permanently (although, since a rule change in 2008, it is only a replica).

If the Champions League and European Cup titles are combined, Real Madrid is the most successful club, with a total of 13 titles (six in the European Cup and seven in the Champions League).

UEFA Champions League timeline:

1955 – The European Cup was established

1992 – The Champions League began

1994 – The Champions League expanded to 16 clubs

1996 – Juventus beat Ajax in the first final to be settled by a penalty shoot-out

1999 – The competition expanded to include 32 clubs

c. Domestic/European International Tournaments

In 1872, the first match between two national teams, England and Scotland, resulted in a 0-0 draw. It was watched by 4,000 spectators at Hamilton Crescent in Scotland. In contrast, Wembley today can seat 90,000 fans.

In 1883, twelve years after football was established as a sport, the first international tournament was held. It comprised four national teams: England, Ireland, Scotland, and Wales. Scotland emerged as the winner of the inaugural competition.

The European Football Championships (known as the Euros) is contested by national teams from Europe. It has taken place every four years since 1960 (missing 2020 due to Covid). In this competition, only the host country automatically qualifies.

The other 23 teams have to compete in a qualifying process involving groups of teams playing home and away in mini-leagues.

d. International World Tournament

The sport's governing body, the Fédération Internationale de Football Association (FIFA), was established in 1904. Representatives from France, Belgium, Denmark, the Netherlands, Spain, Sweden, and Switzerland signed the foundation act. Initially, England and other British territories did not join FIFA. As the 'inventors' of the game, they were resistant to an association having such a key role. However, they joined the following year and participated in the World Cup for the first time in 1950.

No sporting event besides the Summer Olympic Games compares with the World Cup. The first World Cup was played in 1930 in Uruguay, and since then, the Tournament has been played every fourth year except 1942 and 1946 during the Second World War.

Only one team has ever won the World Cup playing in red - England. Despite the popularity of the colour at club level, a team with red as a first-choice strip has yet to win a world title.

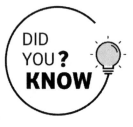
DID YOU? KNOW

The contest starts with a qualification process that takes place over the previous three years to determine which teams will qualify for the Tournament, which is known as The World Cup Finals. Fortunately for some, the host nation and the holders are exempt from this qualification process. Thirty-two international teams compete over a period of a month for the Jules Rimet (former president of the French Football Federation) Cup. Football has undergone significant globalisation since the late 19th century, when only a handful of national teams existed. Today, FIFA has 211 national associations and 200 countries participating in World Cup qualifying, far more than the 32 in 1934. There was no qualification process in 1930.

Every FIFA member association has the opportunity to qualify for the World Cup, and in the 2022 event, Qatar automatically qualified as the host nation. Since the inaugural tournaments held in 1930 and 1934, this was the first time that a country that had never played in a World Cup final before hosted the tournament.

The World Cup is a significant event in football, mainly because there is only one team representing an entire country. While the UEFA Champions League may feature games of similar or even higher quality, it cannot match the status earned by the sport's longest-running international tournament. Viewing figures alone are incomparable. Over three billion television viewers worldwide viewed the latest FIFA World Cup, with one billion watching the final.

Before the World Cup, the football tournament at the Summer Olympics held the most prestige. However, when football transitioned to professional status in the 1920s, this became inconsistent with the then-Olympic spirit, provoking the creation of the World Cup.

19. World Cup Fun Facts

- ★ The 1930 World Cup was played in Uruguay with 13 nations.
- ★ The 1982 World Cup was played in Spain, with 24 nations.
- ★ The 1998 World Cup 1998 was played in France with 32 nations.
- ★ Brazil has won the most World Cups, with five victories.
- ★ The home (host) team has won the competition six times. Teams that don't usually do well in the tournament perform better when hosting it. Sweden, for example, reached the final in 1958, and South Korea reached the semi-finals in 2006.

On both occasions, these countries were the hosts. Neither team has been as successful away from home since.

★ The Jules Rimet Trophy (which is awarded to the winner of the Football World Cup) was on display at a stamp exhibition in central London, however, on Sunday 20th March 1966 it was stolen whilst the Security Guards were on their break. The trophy was soon recovered by a black and white collie dog named Pickles, who was later commended and gained a cult following for his heroism. Despite the trophy being recovered, the FA received a ransom note signed by someone calling himself Jackson. He demanded £15,000 (nearly £250,000 today) for the safe return of the trophy. On the advice of Police, the FA pretended to agree to Jackson's demands and an undercover policeman met Jackson (who turned out to be a former soldier named Edward Betchley) in Battersea Park with a suitcase filled with newspaper covered in a layer of £5 notes. Betchely was then arrested.

★ Players are awarded World Cup Awards, the most notable of which is the Golden Ball, given to the best player. FIFA nominates candidates for this award, and then media representatives choose the winner.

★ Awards are also given to the player who scores the most goals (the Golden Boot) and to the best goalkeeper of the tournament (the Golden Glove).

★ Over the years, the FIFA World Cup tournament prize money has significantly increased. In 1982, the total prize was $20 million; in comparison, the 2022 tournament had a total prize of $440 million, with the winners receiving $42 million.

20. Football Referee and Officials

Football games are officiated by a referee who usually has two assistants known as linesmen. The maximum number of assistant referees per game is two, although Video Assistant Referees (VARs) will provide extra scrutiny during elite games.

21. Drawn Matches and Penalty Shout-Outs

Between 1867 and 1970, there was no definitive way to break ties (drawn results) in football matches. The FA Cup and other early knockout competitions used extra time and replays to determine the winner, while, during the 1920s, specific charity matches utilised corner kicks to break ties and avoid replays. In light of this, the laws of the game were altered in 1923 to specify that only goals would count as points and that any match ending with an equal number of goals would be deemed a draw.

In major competitions, when a replay or playoff was not possible (usually for time constraint reasons), teams drew lots to decide a winner. The most high-profile example was when Italy beat the USSR in the semi-final of the 1968 European Championship. Incidentally, the final was also drawn, but this time, the teams played again two days later, and Italy went on to beat Yugoslavia. In league matches, it is perfectly acceptable for games to end in a draw. However, in knockout competitions, one team must win the match. In most professional competitions, if the score is tied at the end of regulation time (90 minutes), two 15-minute periods of extra time are played before resorting to a penalty shoot-out if necessary.

In 1968, an Israeli team lost an Olympic quarter-final against Bulgaria, which was settled by the drawing of lots. This so incensed Yosef Dagan, the boss of the Israeli FA, that he wrote to FIFA suggesting a five-penalty per team penalty shoot-out, a format which has since been adopted. Penalty shoot-outs can decide which team advances to the next round or ultimately wins the entire competition and are, therefore, a critical part of the modern game.

The first penalty shoot-out in a professional match took place in 1970 during the semi-final of the Watney Cup between Hull City and Manchester United at Boothferry Park in England. Manchester United emerged victorious, with George Best taking the first kick. Ian McKechnie made history as Hull City's goalkeeper by being the first keeper ever to take a penalty kick. Unfortunately, his shot hit the crossbar and deflected over, resulting in Hull City's elimination from the Cup.

What happens during a penalty shoot-out?

During a penalty shoot-out, the manager will select five players to take the team's penalty kicks. The referee will toss a coin to determine which team kicks the first penalty. Then a player from the other team takes one, and this goes on until each team has taken five penalties. The team with the most goals at the end of the shoot-out is declared the winner. Shoot-outs finish as soon as one team has an insurmountable lead. What happens, though, if the scores are level after five pairs of penalties? In that case, the shoot-out progresses into additional 'sudden-death' rounds, where the players continue to kick at goal until one team eventually misses.

Although the procedure for each kick in the shoot-out resembles that of a normal penalty kick, there are some important differences. The main one is that neither the kicker nor any player besides the defending goalkeeper may play the ball again once it has been kicked. In a penalty shoot-out, all players except the kicker and the goalkeepers must stay within the centre circle. The goalkeeper of the kicking team must position themselves at the point where the goal line and the penalty area line (18 yards or 16.5 metres) intersect.

Penalty shoot-out procedure:

- The referee flips a coin to determine which end of the pitch will be used.

- The referee flips another coin to decide which team will take the first penalty.

- During a penalty shoot-out, each penalty is taken like a regular penalty kick from the penalty spot, with only the opposing goalkeeper defending the goal. During a penalty kick, the goalkeeper must stay on the goal line between the goalposts until the ball is kicked. However, they can attempt to distract the penalty taker by jumping, waving their arms, or moving from side to side.

- Before the shoot-out, each team selects the order in which eligible players will take the kicks. If they wish, a manager can substitute a player just before the shoot-out to bring on a specialist penalty taker.

- A goal is scored when the ball crosses the goal line between the posts and under the crossbar after being kicked once and without touching any player besides the goalkeeper.

- Teams take turns kicking until each has taken five. If the score remains tied, sudden-death rounds of one kick each will be used until one team scores and the other misses.

- Only players who were on the pitch or temporarily absent at the end of play are allowed to participate.

- If a goalkeeper is injured, a substitute can replace them during the shoot-out, provided the team has not already used the maximum number of substitutions.

Goalkeepers face the challenging task of defending against penalty kicks. Some decide which way to dive beforehand, while others try to read the kicker's motion pattern. Kickers may attempt to feint or delay their shot to see which way the keeper dives. However, goalkeepers are not allowed to use distracting gamesmanship.

Shoot-Out Fun Facts

★ The 1976 European Championship final between Czechoslovakia and West Germany was the first major international tournament to be decided by a penalty shoot-out. Czechoslovakia won the shoot-out 5–3, with the deciding kick being converted by Antonín Panenka with a 'chip' after Uli Hoeneß had put the previous kick over the bar. The chipped penalty is now known as a Panenka.

★ The first penalty shoot-out in a World Cup took place in 1982. but would not have been used in the final unless the replay was also drawn. Since 1986, penalties have been used for all matches without any possibility of replays.

★ In the 1984 European Cup final, Liverpool beat Roma in the first International Club penalty shoot-out. Liverpool keeper Bruce Grobbelaar gained fame for his antics during the shoot-out, including pretending to eat spaghetti by biting the back of the net.

★ Chelsea won the 2012 Champions League final against Bayern Munich 4-3 on penalties, with Didier Drogba scoring the winning penalty.

★ Penalty shoot-outs have faced criticism for being a lottery rather than a test of skill.

★ There are also claims that the team kicking first has an unfair advantage in penalty shoot-outs, with statistical evidence showing that the team kicking first wins in 60% of cases. This is likely due to the pressure on the team kicking second if they are already behind in the shootout.

★ To prevent a potential first-mover advantage, a new approach called 'ABBA' was suggested. This approach follows the serving sequence in a tennis tiebreak. It involves Team A kicking first, followed by Team B, then Team B, and finally Team A. The ABBA format was used in the 2017 Community Shield shoot-out match between Chelsea and Arsenal, which Arsenal won.

Alternative Methods/Tie-Break Methods

Various other tie-break methods have been proposed before and since shoot-outs were introduced. Other suggestions to overcome tie-breaks include taking into account elements of match play like:

- Most shots on goal
- Most corner kicks awarded

- Fewest cautions and sending-offs
- Or having ongoing extra time with teams compelled to remove players at progressive intervals.
- Another alternative is the Attacker versus Goalkeeper method, which features ten contests where an attacker kicks off from 32 yards (29.3 metres) and has twenty seconds to score a goal against a defender and goalkeeper. The team with the most goals wins at the end of the ten contests.

However, the International Football Association Board has not yet authorised any of these proposals.

22. Role of the Football Manager

The manager, also known as the gaffer in the UK, has complete authority over the team's strategy and playing style.

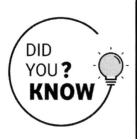

Any players not chosen for the match or not currently on the pitch, sit on the substitute bench. During matches, Coaches and Managers can make five substitutions, however, a Manager can only use their substitutions in batches of three. Usually this means substituting two players to begin with, then another two later and then the fifth and final substitute whenever they're needed.

During the match, the manager is limited to their 'dugout' and a 'technical area', which is a dotted line extending one metre on either side of the designated seated area and forward up to a distance of 75 cm from the touchline. In drawn knock-out matches, Managers are only allowed onto the pitch after 90 minutes have elapsed to discuss tactics with their players.

Substitutions are a great way to change the game. It gives the Manager a chance to change the tactics or take a player off who is not at the top of their game. However, once a player leaves the pitch, they cannot come back on under any circumstances. If the manager wants to start pushing for a win, they might want to remove a defender and substitute with an attacking player. If the goalkeeper gets injured or is issued a red card and is sent off, the Manager will bring on a new keeper and sacrifice an outfield player.

23. Fun Football Quotes

Bobby Robson

"The first 90 minutes are the most important."

Michael Owen

"I don't believe in superstitions. I just do certain things because I'm scared in case something will happen if I don't do them."

Bill Shankly

"Aim for the sky and you'll hit the ceiling. Aim for the ceiling and you'll stay on the floor."

Brian Clough

"Believe it or not, cricket was my first love. I would genuinely have swapped the dream of winning a goal at Wembley for a century against the Australians at Lords."

Brian Clough - on listening to player's opinions

"We talk about it for 20 minutes and then we decide I was right."

24. Common Footballing Terminology

★ A clean sheet – when a team doesn't concede any goals in a game.

★ A dead ball specialist – describes a player who is particularly skilful at striking a stationary ball, such as a free kick.

★ A hospital pass – when a player passes the ball to a teammate in such a way that it is difficult for them to keep possession.

★ A nutmeg – when a player kicks the ball through the legs of an opponent.

★ Hitting the woodwork – the ball has hit the post or crossbar. It is a throwback to when goalposts were made of wood.

★ A professional foul – when a player deliberately obstructs an opponent to prevent a goal from being scored. This is punished by a yellow or red card.

Chapter Four

GOLF

"Golf is the closest game to the game we call life. You get bad breaks from good shots; you get good breaks from bad shots - but you have to play the ball where it lies."

Bobby Jones

CONTENTS

1. What is Golf?

Golf is a sport in which players use various clubs to hit a small ball from a *tee* to a hole on a fine cut, putting green in as few shots as possible. The first shot is played by placing the ball on a small peg known as a tee, and the second from wherever the first lands. The last shot is when the ball finally lays to rest in the small hole on the putting green. Unlike most sports, Golf does not use a standardised playing area and coping with the varied terrains encountered on different courses is a vital part of the game. There can be several different terrains between the tee and the green (where the hole is located), such as the fairway (good) and the rough (bad), along with various hazards, such as water, trees and bunkers that are filled with sand.

2. Basic Equipment

- Golf club – a metal stick with a metal head.
- Golf balls - these are a core of rubber covered by a resin called Surlyn or Urethane which is an artificial compound also used in pesticides. Golf balls have dimples on their surface to help increase the lift and reduce drag. Interestingly, the number of dimples on a golf ball can vary from around 300 to over 500, with the precise arrangement of the dimples affecting the ball's flight.
- Ball marker – for marking the position of a ball on the green.
- Tees – for putting a golf ball on at the beginning of each hole.
- Golf bag – for holding clubs, balls, tees and other paraphernalia.
- Golf shoes – to wear. These are strong enough to stop feet from moving whilst swinging the club and have spikes on the soles to prevent slipping on the green.
- Glove – to wear on one hand. Golfers wear one glove on their weaker hand to provide a better grip on the club.
- Scorecard – to record the number of shots played per hole.
- Dodgy clothing ??

The equipment used in golf has undergone many changes and improvements over time. The golf ball, for example, evolved considerably until the 1930s when the United States Golf Association (USGA) established weight and size standards. Since 1990, regulations have dictated that a golf ball must be at least 1.68 inches (4.26 cm) in diameter and weigh no more than 1.62 ounces (44.9 grams).

Golf Clubs

If you are new to golf, you might wonder what the different clubs are used for. Put simply, there are four types of clubs, explained as follows:

1. **Drivers and Woods** are designed to hit the ball the farthest. Although woods were initially made from hard woods such as beech, they are now made from metal or composite materials. These clubs are the longest in the golf bag and are used for the first shot taken on each hole (except for the short holes). There are generally three kinds of wood, numbered one, three, and five, with slightly different degrees of angle (to affect the height of the shot).

2. **Irons** come in various lengths and are designed for shots requiring more precision. Their flat faces result in shots that don't travel as far but stop more quickly upon landing. Traditionally, Irons are labelled from one to nine (longest to shortest), and a good player will know precisely how far each club will hit the ball. A player may, for example, know that their six iron will hit the ball 180 yards, with the difference between each iron being, on average, a distance of 10 yards. The difference between a two-iron and a nine-iron could easily be 70 yards due to the tilt and angle of the club head. Before choosing a club to play, players will also consider the strength and direction of the wind and whether they are hitting the ball up or downhill.

3. **Wedges** are irons with a much larger angle and are the shortest clubs in the golf bag. When a player uses a wedge, the ball travels much higher but far shorter. They are used to hit the ball a short distance as the player nears the hole. If a ball lands in a sandy bunker, players will use a sand wedge to retrieve it.

4. **Putters** are used when the ball is on the green, and the final shots are needed to sink it into the hole. The putter has a straight face and is considered the most important club in the bag—after all, about half of all golf shots are made with it. It is perhaps the reason someone coined the phrase, "Golfers drive for show, but putt for dough."

A player is limited to having 14 clubs in their golf bag, which typically includes one driver, a three- and/or five-wood, eight irons, two or three wedges, and one putter.

3. The History of the Game

The origins of golf are a topic of much debate and uncertainty, but it is widely accepted that modern golf originated in Scotland during the Middle Ages. The game didn't gain global popularity until the late 19th century, though, when it expanded to the rest of the United Kingdom, the British Empire, and, eventually, the United States.

According to records, the earliest 'known' game was played on February 26, 1297, in Loenen aan de Vecht in the Netherlands. Played using a stick and a leather ball; the objective was to hit the ball with the fewest strokes into a target located hundreds of yards away. The winner was determined by the player who played the least number of strokes.

Early Golf in Scotland

Stick and ball games have existed for centuries, though we are pretty sure that the modern game we see today had its roots in Scotland. The word golf is believed to be a Scottish variation of the Dutch words 'colf' or 'colve,' which means 'stick' or 'club'.

The Old Course at St. Andrews, near Edinburgh, Scotland, is the oldest golf course in the world, with records dating back to the 15th Century.

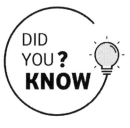

The first documented reference to golf in Scotland came in an Act of Parliament in 1457. In this Act, King James II issued a proclamation banning golf and football from being played as they distracted from archery practice that was being undertaken for military purposes. Further bans were ordered in 1471 and 1491, with golf then being regarded as an 'unprofitable sport'.

When King James IV came to the throne, he too banned golf, although clubs and balls were purchased for him in 1502 on his visit to Perth. He also had these items purchased when he was in St Andrews and Edinburgh. In total, the game was banned three times during a thirty-four-year period, which means the Scottish courts were exceedingly busy repealing all those Acts!

The spread of the game

In 1603, James VI of Scotland succeeded to the throne of England. His son, the Prince of Wales (the future King Charles 1, who was later beheaded by Oliver Cromwell) and his courtiers played golf at Blackheath, London, where the Royal Blackheath Golf Club traces its origins. Evidence shows that Scottish soldiers, expatriates and immigrants took the game to British colonies and elsewhere during the 18th century with the Royal Calcutta Golf Club (1829), the Mauritius Gymkhana Club (1844), and the club at Pau (1856) in south-western France being notable reminders of these excursions. Outside of the British Isles, these three clubs are the oldest recorded.

DID YOU **?** **KNOW**

On December the 10th, 1659, an order was issued to prevent golf from being played in the streets of Albany, New York. This was because too many windows were being broken!

In 1681, James V1 of Scotland, the then Duke of Albany, was said to have played the first international golf match. He and two English courtiers competed as part of a wager over who had the right to claim the game for Scotland or England. His partner, John Paterson, was paid enough money to build a mansion in the area of Edinburgh now known as Golfers Land.

The late 19th Century boom

In the 1850s, Queen Victoria and Prince Albert built Balmoral Castle in the Scottish Highlands. With the railways reaching St Andrews in 1852, by the 1860s, there were fast and regular services between London and Edinburgh. The royal enthusiasm for Scotland, the much-improved transport links and the writings of Sir Walter Scott caused a boom in tourism in Scotland and a wider interest in Scottish history and culture. This led to golf spreading across the rest of the British Isles. In 1864, the golf course at the resort of Westward Ho! in Devon became the first

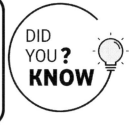

Alan Shephard, an astronaut on the Apollo 14 Space Mission, hit two golf balls whilst on the moon. The balls travelled for several hundred yards due to the low gravity on the moon.

DID YOU **?** KNOW

new club in England since Blackheath in 1603. By 1880, England had twelve courses, which rose to fifty in 1887 and over 1,000 by 1914. The popularity of golf also spread throughout the British Empire, with clubs being established in Ireland, Australia, New Zealand, Canada, and South Africa.

4. Types of Golf Courses

The most well-known type of golf course is a **Links Course**, but there are others. The term 'links' refers to a type of course originating from the Old English word 'hlinc', which means rising ground or ridge. These courses are found mainly in Scotland, Ireland and England and are characterised by their location near the coast and the fact they are built on sandy soil. The benefit of this sandy soil is that it provides excellent drainage, making the ground firm and ideal for golf. Many courses may claim to be links style or have 'links' in their name, but only those which meet these specific criteria (coastal location and sandy soil) can be considered true links courses. When the game began gaining popularity, the use of this land was suggested, given its unsuitability for agriculture. Some of the most famous links courses include The Old Course at St. Andrews and the course at Royal Troon.

Another type of course is the **Parkland Course**, which is built inland and away from the sea. These courses are known for their trees and lush grass, hence their name, and usually incorporate artificial features such as ponds. It is (oddly) typical for these courses to be built in areas not ideally suited to golf, which results in more problematic grass and soil. The maintenance costs are thus significantly higher, and it is more challenging for course architects to add intrigue and excitement to these courses since there is less natural land movement and undulation. Augusta National in Georgia, USA, is arguably the most well-known parkland course in the World, not least because it is where the Masters (one of the most prestigious tournaments in the World) is held every April.

The third type of course is the **Heathland Course**, which is defined as an open, uncultivated area of land with heather, gorse and coarse grasses, typically found in Britain. Heathland Courses are usually more open than Parkland Courses and are designed to resemble Links Courses since they were created as an alternative to Links Courses when people sought additional golfing options. The terrain of a Heathland Course is often undulating with sandy soil and many of Britain's top-rated golf courses are heathland, including Gleneagles in Scotland.

<u>Why are there 18 holes on a Golf Course?</u>

At its inception, there was no standard length for a game of golf. In the 1700s, Leith and Bruntsfield Links Courses had five holes, whilst St Andrews had eleven. These eleven were played twice (out and back), which made a full round of twenty-two. In 1764, the St Andrews Links Course was altered, and the first four holes were merged into two longer ones. After that, the course was nine holes out and nine holes back, and with St Andrews having been established as golf's home by that point, a round of eighteen holes stuck.

5. Etiquette

Golf is a sport that emphasizes etiquette and proper behaviour. Observing good etiquette shows respect for the game, fellow players, and the golf course, and meaningful traditions have been established over the years, including shaking hands with your opponents at the first tee and last hole.

Some general examples of etiquette are:

i. Respect the course, which means treating it with care and respect. Players are expected to repair divots (marks made in the grass by golfers as they play), replace or fill in ball marks on the greens, and rake bunkers after playing a shot.

ii. The players toss a coin to determine who plays the first shot of a round. After each player has played their first shot, the one whose ball is furthest from the hole plays next, i.e. the player who has hit the ball the shortest distance. This order of play continues (with the furthest going next and so on) until all players have completed the hole. As odd as it sounds, it is quite possible for one golfer to be playing their fourth shot before another has played their second. When all players have successfully putted their balls into the hole, the player who won the hole (completed it in the fewest shots) becomes the first player for the next hole. This continues until a different player wins a hole. The player who takes the first shot is thus said to 'have the honour'.

iii. Whether the flag should remain in the hole has been a topic of debate for centuries. The purpose of the flag is to enable players to see the hole from a distance; however, when it comes to putting, if the flag remains in place, it can cause a deflection with the ball ricocheting in an unexpected direction. It used to always be the case, therefore, that the flag had to be removed. The rules on this were updated in 2019, though, so that players can now leave the flag in place if they wish, whereas before, any player forgetting to remove it would have incurred a penalty shot.

If one golf ball hits another, the outcome of these two balls colliding depends on where the collision occurred. If it happens **off the green,** the ball that has been hit must be returned to its original resting position and the ball which struck the other one, has to be played from where it came to rest. There is no penalty.

If, however, the collision happens **on the green**, the player hitting the striking ball incurs a two-shot penalty as this could be considered a deliberate ploy to knock an opponent's ball off line. The striking ball is then played from where it ended up, and the moved ball will return to its original resting position.

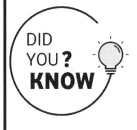

6. The Most Important Rules of the Game

i. Clubs in the bag

Players may only carry fourteen clubs in their bag during a competitive round and there is a penalty should they carry more. As an example, during the 2001 Open Championship, overnight leader Ian Woosnam was penalised two additional strokes for having one club too many in his bag. In games that are closely contested (such as the Open Championship), such a deficit can be huge and difficult to claw back. Ian Woosman would end up tying for third place.

Hugh Campbell, chairman of the championship committee, commented that Woosnam was late arriving at the first tee, which could have accounted for the error.

"Ian got to the first tee about thirty seconds before he was due to start," Campbell said. *"Some players like to leave it that late rather than hang around waiting to play, but it means there isn't time for the usual conversation between the official and the player or his caddie."*

Campbell went on to explain that players usually ask their caddies to check the number of clubs just in case an extra one has been put in there by mistake, but as Woosnam was late to the tee, this conversation may not have happened.

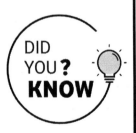

DID YOU **?** **KNOW**

Golfers shout the word 'fore!' to warn other players that their ball is headed towards them so that the other player can move out of the line of the ball and avoid being hit! We are unsure of the origins of this phrase, but a common theory is that the term originated from the word 'forecaddie' who was a person tasked with walking ahead of the players to spot where their balls had landed. If a ball being played then headed in the direction of this 'forecaddie', the word 'forecaddie' would have been shouted in warning which has, over time, been shortened to the word 'fore'.

ii. Play within the parameters of the tee

The first tee shot of a round is always daunting, even for experienced players. The tee and shot must be taken within marked parameters (usually white markers for tournaments, yellow for men's games and red for ladies' games), and there is a two-stroke penalty if you take your first shot from outside of these markers

iii. Avoid playing the wrong ball

This might sound obvious, but unless players mark their ball before they start, there's a danger of players mistaking their ball for another player's. As playing the wrong golf ball comes with a two-shot penalty, golfers often mark their balls with distinctive personalised symbols. One golfer, Tommy Fleetwood from England, draws a smiley face on his ball, for example, to make sure he doesn't inadvertently hit the wrong one.

iv. Play the ball as it lies

Unless the rules state otherwise, balls must always be played as they lie (i.e., where they land). Even if your ball is moved by natural forces like wind or water, you must still play it from its resting spot.

v. Green rulings

Once a player reaches the green, there are a couple of further considerations:

- When the ball comes to rest on a putting green, players can lift it for cleaning, but they must mark its location with a coin or a disk. The ball must be replaced in exactly the same spot.
- Golfers are permitted to repair almost any damage on the green, such as spike marks, ball marks, indentations from a club or flag or animal damage. They are not, however, permitted to repair aeration holes, natural surface imperfections, or the natural wear of the hole.

vi. No way back from out of bounds (OB)

If a ball ends up in an out-of-bounds area, the shot must be replayed from the original starting position, and a one-stroke penalty is added. Players have a maximum of three minutes to search for their ball and/or they can continue with a new ball, known as a provisional ball, providing they notify the other players of their intention. If a ball is lost, it can be beneficial for a player to go straight to a provisional ball to save valuable time. However, its use does incur a one-stroke penalty. If the original ball is found, then it must be played but with no penalty.

vii. Seeking advice

Players may ask for advice on topics such as club selection, but only from their caddie or teammates. Information regarding rules, distances, positions of hazards or the flag, however, may be requested from others

viii. Definition of ball striking

Striking the ball may seem like a matter of technique, but it is also partly governed by the rules. For instance, if a player finds themselves in a difficult position with an awkward stance, they must still hit the ball with the head of the club. A two-shot penalty can be given if the player spoons, scrapes, or flicks the ball in a style which cannot be described as a 'stroke'.

ix. Score correctly

Players must ensure their scorecard has been completed correctly at the end of a round. Cards are exchanged at the beginning of each round for the players to log both their own and their opponent's scores. At the end, cards are returned to their original owner and scores are compared. Once all players agree then the cards must be signed (by all), noting it as a correct record of each hole. Incorrect or unsigned scorecards will lead to disqualification.

At the 2000 Benson and Hedges International Open, Irish golfer Padraig Harrington (who would go on to win the Open Championship in 2007 and 2008) was disqualified five minutes before teeing off on the final round despite having a five-shot lead simply because he hadn't 't signed his scorecard correctly.

7. Playing the Game (Strokeplay)

You may have heard the term 'par for the course'. This refers to the number of shots a professional player is expected to play during a round. For some courses, this is 70 shots, some 73 and some in-between. Each of the 18 holes has its own 'expected' score; for example, a par four hole would have an expected score of four shots. If you hit more than four shots on the hole, you are said to be 'over par', and if you hit less than four, you will be 'under par'. In most tournaments, the player with the lowest score (the fewest number of strokes) after four rounds wins the tournament.

You may also hear references to the following:

- A **birdie** - a score of one under par on a hole (for example, scoring four on a par five).
- A **bogey** is one over par.
- An **eagle** is two under par.
- A **double bogey** is two over par.

Where did the term 'birdie' come from though?

In his book *Fifty Years Of American Golf, H.B. Martin* revealed that when golfers struck a ball well, their playing partners would say, "What a bird of a shot." At the time, no specific terms were associated with one or two under par. However, over time, a birdie was assigned to a score of one shot fewer than par. One theory suggests that players called two under par an eagle because it is bigger than other birds.

This is a typical golf card for the first nine holes of a course (explanation on following page).

Hole	Distance (yds)	Par	Stroke Index	Score (Shots)
1	423	4	4	
2	496	5	5	
3	374	4	2	
4	432	4	7	
5	145	3	3	
6	432	4	6	
7	532	5	8	
8	397	4	1	
9	186	3	9	
TOTAL	3426	36		

- Column 1 – holes are played in a pre-determined order arranged by the course designer. For convenience, the first and ninth (as well as the tenth and eighteenth) are usually near the Clubhouse.
- Column 2 - shows the length of the hole (from tee to centre of the green) in yards.
- Column 3 - shows the expected number of shots to get the ball from the tee to the hole. Players are assumed to take two shots (putts) whilst on the green, plus several shots added for the distance between the tee and the green.
- Column 4 - ranks the hole in order of difficulty to attain the par number of shots. So, in the example above, the eighth is considered the hardest with the ninth, the easiest.
- Column 5 - is where the number of shots taken by a player is recorded.

The honour of the longest golf hole belongs to the THIRD at Gunsan Coun Jeolla, South Korea, which measures 1,097 yards.

Handicaps

Golf has designed a way of allowing two players of different abilities to play a round of golf and still give them each an equal chance of winning. This system incorporates the use of a handicap which is a number of shots allowance given to each player depending upon their skill level. Stronger players have lower handicaps and less experienced players will have higher handicaps. The system works by the player with the lower handicap 'giving' several shots equal to the difference in their handicaps to the other player. So, if one player has a handicap of three and the other's handicap is fourteen, the former 'gives' up eleven shots. The way it works in practice is that the weaker player deducts one shot on the most challenging (in this example) eleven holes. If the difference is more than eighteen, then multiple shots can be deducted at each hole.

The maximum handicap for men is 28, and for women, it is 36.

8. Tactics/Styles

Imagine you are on the first tee of a golf course, which is usually situated near the car park, the professional shop and, most importantly, the clubhouse. This means people may be watching as you prepare. As you are considering your shot, the first decision to make is which club to use. The one you ultimately decide upon depends upon the following factors:

a. The length of the hole
b. Your confidence
c. Where do you want the ball to land? (More on this later in 'Key Decisions')

Once you've taken that first shot, you move to wherever your ball lands in readiness for your next one.

There is an expression to describe how fortunate or otherwise a player is once the ball has landed. If their next shot is considered to be '*easy*', then the term '*a good lie*' may be used. Conversely, if the ball has landed behind a tree or on rough terrain, the player is said to have a '*bad lie*' because their next shot is likely to be more difficult.

When you get to about 100 yards from the hole, you will find yourself close to the (putting) green–the closely cropped grass with the hole and the flag in the hole. At this point, you need to consider where on the green you want your ball to land to give the best chance of putting the ball into the hole.

When you reach the green, it's time to putt the ball, taking care to get the angle and strength with which you hit the ball just right. This decision can be helped if you 'read' the green well – do you expect the ball to move from left to right or vice versa, for example?

When it comes to putting, I always remember the advice I was once given by a professional golfer. He suggested considering how water might flow if a bucket were tipped over and aiming your ball accordingly.

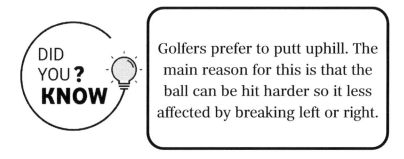

DID YOU? KNOW

Golfers prefer to putt uphill. The main reason for this is that the ball can be hit harder so it less affected by breaking left or right.

A typical golf green

Size of a golf hole

Until it was standardised in 1891, a golf hole could be any size. As crazy as it sounds, a rabbit hole could suffice, or a landowner could randomly dig a hole of any dimension. As a result, many courses had a variety of different sized holes on their course. In 1829, a golf course at Musselburgh began to use a standardised hole of four and a quarter inches, but it took a long time for this to spread to the rest of the world.

Bunkers

Golf course designers try to reward good shots, punish poor ones, and allow golfers to take calculated risks. With this in mind, bunkers and other hazards are always carefully placed by the designer.

The average professional golfer only beats par on fewer than four holes per round of golf.

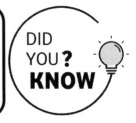
DID YOU? KNOW

Ideally, players want their ball to land on the fairway or green so that their next shot is as easy as possible. However, if they take a risk which doesn't pay off, their ball may land in a sandy bunker. This automatically makes their next shot a lot more challenging. Hitting a shot from the sand is different from hitting one from the grass. When playing shots from bunkers, players need to apply a whole other skill set, special techniques, and specialist clubs; otherwise, they can find themselves stuck in the bunker for a long time.

9. Key Decisions

It's easy to think that (professional) golfers hit good shots most of the time, particularly if you watch coverage of the major tournaments; however, this is not necessarily true. Crucially, in addition to being able to hit the ball well, they also have the ability to manage risk. A successful golfer once stated that the 'art of winning tournament golf is to understand when to defend as well as when to attack'.

Prior to any tournament, golfers will have been able to play a practice round, and from this, they are able to deduce which holes give them the best opportunity to outscore their rivals. They will also be able to work out which holes are going to give them the most difficulty. With this information in mind, the golfer will manage their strategy and work out a plan of how to play every one of the eighteen holes.

How to form a strategy:

1. Consider where to hit the tee shot. This might seem obvious - surely, players will aim to hit the ball in a straight line as far as possible – however, it's not that simple. Players need to have a plan for where they want every shot to land. When they play their first shot (known as their tee shot), they will want to consider their second shot and play for that. The aerial picture of a golf hole below is a great illustration of this. This is a par four hole of 450 yards (distance), so the consideration is whether to hit the ball over the lake (adventurous) or aim straight (the more cautious approach).

3D mock-up of overhead view of a typical golf hole - AI generated elements

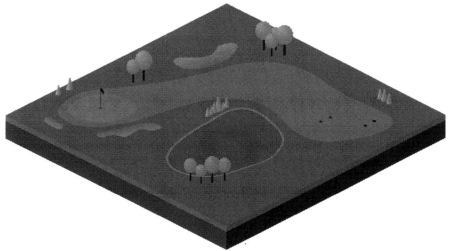

2. Decide which club to use. Players will know how far they can hit the ball with each club, so they will take this into account when selecting one.

3. Then, it's a case of thinking about the lay of the land. Is it uphill or downhill, and which way is the wind blowing and at what speed? These factors will all affect how hard to hit the ball and in which direction.

4. Often, the distance to the target does not match the distance the player can hit the ball; therefore, they need to work out whether they should hit 'long' or 'short' and what the implications of both are. Will they land in the rough, for example, if they hit too short? Golfers will practice their swing before every shot which is an important part of their strategy. It enables them to focus their mind on the precise objective of that shot.

5. When putting, the two key considerations are the distance to the hole (which determines how hard to hit the ball) and the direction the ball needs to travel (which tells them where to aim). Although they might look it, greens are never flat, so the player must decide which side of the hole to hit towards so that the ball will roll into the hole.

Even with a great strategy, players are always having to balance risk with reward, calculating what the likely outcome will be for each shot. There is also a mental strategy to the game. It was once reported that Tiger Woods would ask his opponents if they breathed in or out when they swung or when they putted. By making them think about this – which is not something they would have usually considered – they became more aware of their breathing, often to the detriment of their game.

It is important to bear in mind that as players have to play all shots (except for the tee shot) from where the previous shot landed, no two shots are precisely the same. Every time a player approaches their ball then, there is a new situation to evaluate.

10. Factors Affecting the Location of the Hole

Tournament officials must decide where on the green to put the hole. This is known as setting the pin position. In order to do this, they need to consider the type of shot that a player is likely to play when trying to land their ball on the green. The goal is for the shot to be challenging but fair, so the aim is to put the hole in such a place where good shots are rewarded.

The length of the expected approach shot is also taken into account, with officials ensuring that there is enough putting distance around the hole. For instance, if a long iron is needed for the approach shot, the hole will be positioned further from the edge of the green than if a more lofted club is likely to be used. Additionally, weather conditions are considered. A wet green will result in less ball roll than a dry one. According to the rules, holes should be situated at least four paces away from any edge of the putting green and even farther away if a bunker is nearby or if the area surrounding the green slopes downward.

The position of the hole will be different for each of the four rounds of a tournament, and although the officials may choose the positions before the tournament begins, they know that they may have to be flexible in certain weather conditions.

What the flags mean (in relation to the position of the hole)

- If the hole is near the front of the green – the flag is **red**.
- If the hole is near the back of the green – the flag is **blue** or **yellow**.
- If the hole is near the middle of the green – the flag is **white**.

11. Competitions

Most tournaments take place over four days. On the first two days, all players play two rounds of eighteen holes, usually in groups of three. The groups for the second round are the same as the first, regardless of how well or poorly each player scores in the first round. After the first two rounds, a number of players are eliminated from the tournament, which is referred to as 'making' or 'missing' the cut.

12. Golf Caddies

A golf caddie is a person who accompanies a golfer around the course, primarily carrying the golfer's clubs in a bag. They are often experienced players themselves and will offer advice and support throughout.

The caddies for top players get paid a percentage of the player's winnings. If their player wins a tournament, a caddy can earn up to 10% of the players' winnings. To earn this money a caddy has to perform many duties, all of which are designed to help their player to win the tournament.

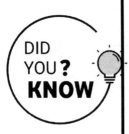

There is some debate about the history of golf caddies. One theory states that in the 15th century, Mary, Queen of Scots, coined the term. She was studying in France and saw French military cadets carrying golf clubs for the Queen. On her return to Scotland, Mary brought the custom of using cadets with her, and the name eventually shortened to caddies. This version is one of the most popular since Queen Mary was the first known woman to play golf.

The key responsibilities of caddies:

i. Hand clubs to the golfer

The caddy is responsible for handing the right golf club to the golfer. They may discuss the distance, wind strength and direction and where they want the ball to land between them, but once this conversation ends, the caddy will hand the chosen club to the player and walk away.

ii. Keep the golf clubs and equipment clean

The caddy is expected to keep the golf clubs, balls, and other equipment clean throughout the round. They should carry towels and appropriate cleaning products with them. It is not uncommon for caddies to ensure the ball is cleaned prior to each tee shot and before each putt.

iii. Have sufficient knowledge of golf

Caddies need to know golfing terminology and the rules of the sport. They must be prepared to provide advice to golfers when asked.

iv. Know the golf course well

Caddies need to know the course well. They will usually walk around it before the tournament begins so that they know the 'lay of the land'. They will also note potential hazards and areas that are out of bounds.

v. Know the distances to the greens

Golfers will frequently ask their caddies how far their ball is from the green and/or the flag. Caddies will use the various distance markers on the course to calculate the distance from ball to green or hole. Some caddies use measuring gadgets which automatically calculate distances.

vi. Rake and bunkers

Caddies are tasked with cleaning up after their golfer when they need to hit their ball out of a bunker. The bunker must be left in the same condition as it was before the golfer entered, so the caddie will rake over the entire area the golfer disturbed.

vii. Fix and replace any ball marks and divots the golfer makes

Caddies are also responsible for tidying up any other mess that golfers leave behind, such as divots on the fairway or marks on the green made by a ball landing from a height.

viii. Watch the ball when it is hit

Caddies need to follow the flight of the ball once it has been struck. They need to know precisely where it landed and, to avoid penalties, they must take their golfer to exactly the right spot.

ix. Become familiar with the golfer's style of play

Caddies need to know the personality and style of the player they are caddying for. In time, the two can develop a close relationship, which can be very useful to a player. Caddies will understand when to calm a player down, when to encourage them and how to get the best out of them, for example.

x. Count the clubs and count again

The last thing a caddy wants is for their golfer to call for a club that is not in the bag. They must take the time to count the clubs and verify each one is present and accounted for. Then, count them a second time just to be safe!

13. The Major Tournaments (known as The Majors)

The most prestigious annual events in Golf are the major tournaments, which are held annually from April to July. Three of these championships are held in America, whilst the oldest and final one is in the UK. These events hold immense prestige and offer substantial prize money.

I.   The Masters (USA)

The Masters is held at the Augusta National Golf Club in Georgia, USA, in April each year. Originally founded by legendary golfer Bobby Jones and investment banker Clifford Roberts, it was first played in 1934 and is unique in that:

- It is the only major to be played on the same course every year.
- A special par three tournament is held before the main event. Many players participate, but no one who has won the par three event has ever gone on to win the main event.
- There is a special dinner for the players the night before the tournament at which the previous winner gets to choose the menu. For example, when Nick Faldo won it, he chose fish and chips for the dinner the following year.
- The winner is awarded the famous Green Jacket. The winner from the previous year presents the new champion with the jacket.
- The winner becomes an honorary member of the (Augusta National Golf) club.

Some unusual features about the Masters:

- Spectators are not known as spectators but as patrons.
- Mobile phones are not allowed on the course.
- There are no large screens around the course, so it can be difficult for patrons to be aware of which players are contending for the title and keep up to date with play.
- All the caddies at the Masters wear white jumpsuits, tennis shoes, and green caps
- Television cables are buried under the fairways to avoid obstructing views of the course.

Unfortunately, Augusta is a club for members only, and unless you're as famous or wealthy as Bill Gates or former Secretary of State Condoleezza Rice—who are both members—your chances of playing on the exclusive course are slim. For the majority of us, the closest we'll ever get to the stunning azaleas that grace the immaculate fairways is from buying tickets to be spectators or patrons.

II.   PGA Championship (USA)

The PGA Championship is played in May and is the second major of the year. Unlike the Masters, it is played on various courses around the US, although it is predominantly staged on the East Coast.

Unlike the other Majors, this competition does not include top amateur golfers – it is open to Pro players only. The winning golfer receives a trophy named after Rodman Wanamaker, who was a prominent figure in the New York City department store industry. He donated the impressive silverware, which is a trophy weighing over 34 pounds (15 kilos) and measuring over 27 inches (86 cm) from handle to handle. From 1916 to 1959, the trophy was engraved with the winner's club or residence; however, since 1960, it has been engraved with the current champion's name and the location of the tournament. Today, the winner receives a replica of the original Wanamaker trophy because the original is now on permanent display at the PGA gallery in Florida. In addition, they receive a smaller replica, which they are permitted to keep.

The trophy went missing for two years between 1928 and 1930. After winning the 1928 tournament, Walter Hagen asked a taxi driver to drop it off at his hotel and it never arrived. It was eventually found in the factory where Hagen was having his own brand of clubs manufactured!

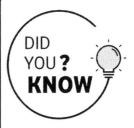
DID YOU? KNOW

III.   US Open (USA)

The third major of the year is the US Open Championship, which always takes place in June and finishes on the same weekend as Father's Day. In 2013, Englishman Justin Rose won the tournament (his first and only major), and on securing victory on Father's Day, he pointed towards the sky and said, "Yes". He later announced that the look up to the skies was for his dad, who had been hugely influential in Rose's career and had sadly died from cancer eleven years earlier. The venue for the event changes from year to year and is traditionally known as the toughest of all four majors due to the conditions (and challenges) of the course(s).

IV.   The Open Championship (UK)

The final golfing major of the year is held in July. The Open Championship, also known as the Open or The British Open, is the only major held outside of America. It is also the oldest golf tournament in the World and is played on a rotation of ten of the finest coastal links courses in the UK. It gets its name from being 'open' to all competitors (both professional and amateur); however, in practice, this is not the case, and only a select few of the leading amateur players are invited to take part.

The first Open was played in 1860 in Scotland and was won by the Scot Willie Park Sr. He was presented with a boxing-style belt known as the 'Challenge Belt', which was donated by the Earl of Eglinton. The winner of the event was also named 'Champion Golfer of the Year', a coveted title that is still used today and sought after by every professional golfer. In 1872, the famous Claret Jug was introduced as the trophy, along with a winner's medal. Both of which are still handed out to the victor today.

Because **links** courses are close to the coast, the wind can often play an integral part in the competition by changing speed and direction, sometimes several times a day. Players must, therefore, be flexible and able to adapt to these changing conditions. The greens at the Open are also the slowest of all four majors due to the threat of the high winds moving their golf balls.

Major Consistencies

Aspects that are consistent across all majors:

- They all start on a Thursday morning and finish on a Sunday evening.
- On each day, a full round of eighteen holes is played (unless weather interferes).
- Before the tournaments begin, a draw takes place to determine who plays with whom.

AI representation of (part of) Augusta National Golf Course

- Up to 156 players will play on Thursday and Friday, with the number of competitors approximately halved for the last two days. Each tournament has its own rules, but typically, players within ten shots of the leader are permitted to play at the weekend.
- For those fortunate enough to make it to the weekend, the groups are reduced to two players, with their order of play determined by their scores for the first two days. Thus, the players with the fewest shots start their rounds last.

Who qualifies to play in the majors?

In the Masters, between 85 and 100 players are 'invited' to compete. This includes the top fifty ranked players as of January 1st, along with players who make it to that same top fifty in the week before the competition begins. Past champions of the Masters and past winners of the other three major tournaments also receive an invitation. The committee can also invite anyone they believe warrants a place.

In the other three major tournaments, 156 players compete, and each one has its own qualifying rules. They also have their own application of the 'cut' to work out which players progress to the weekend (rounds three and four):

1. The Masters – the 50 with the fewest shots plus those on the same score
2. The PGA Championship – the top 70 plus those on the same score
3. The US Open – the top 60 plus those on the same score
4. The Open Championship –the top 70 plus those on the same score

14. How to Win (in the event of a tie)

If two or more players are tied at the end of a 72-hole tournament, a playoff takes place between all those who are tied.

However, the method chosen to determine the eventual winner is not consistent across all tournaments, particularly the four majors:

I. <u>The Masters</u>

This is fairly simple. Any players sharing the lead after 72 holes will play in a sudden death format. They alternate between playing the 18th and 10th holes until a winner emerges. Although these are two great holes (on an amazing course), it's a pretty boring playoff structure.

II. <u>The PGA Championship</u>

All players who are tied at the end of the PGA Championship will take part in a three-hole playoff. If players are still tied after those three holes, they will continue playing hole-by-hole in a sudden-death format until there is a winner.

III.   The US Open

Until 2018, when the rules were changed, all players with the joint lowest score after 72 holes had to come back the next day to play another full round to determine the winner. In an attempt to help players, organisers, television companies and spectators, the rules were then changed. Now, any players tied after 72 holes play the first and eighteenth holes to decide the winner. If the players still can't be separated, they enter sudden death over the same two holes until one eventually wins.

IV.   The Open Championship

Similar to the PGA, at the Open Championship any golfers tied for the lead at the end of 72 holes play a three-hole play playoff. Whoever has the lowest total score for those three holes combined will be the winner. In the event that players are still tied after the playoff, they will continue to play a hole-by-hole sudden-death format until someone eventually wins a hole. The choice of which three holes is made after the organisers have chosen the venue, so it will differ each year.

15. The Ryder Cup

The Ryder Cup began in 1927 and was played at the Worcester Golf Club in Massachusetts. Initially, it was played between two teams, one from the USA and one from Great Britain. However, interest in the tournament dropped when the USA consistently won. In 1979, a decision was made to expand the British team to include players from continental Europe. Since then, the USA team has won nine matches, and the European team has won twelve.

For many casual fans, the Ryder Cup is often their 'introduction' to the Sport and is different from most other tournaments the top players enter:

- Unlike all other tournaments, the Ryder Cup is played every two years, alternating between courses in the USA and in Europe.
- Players form a team of twelve either from their country (the United States) or their continent (Europe).
- Matches are played using a match play format as opposed to stroke play (see explanation below).
- Each team has a (non-playing) captain and a number of vice-captains.

- The two teams have their own methods for player selection (mostly by pre-agreed qualification formula such as world ranking), though the captains are also able to choose some players.

- The Ryder Cup is played over three days, starting on Friday morning and ending on Sunday evening.

- There is no prize money for winning The Ryder Cup.

What is Matchplay?

Hole Number(s)	Player A's Score	Player B's Score	Score (Player A's perspective)
1	4	5	1 Up
2-8	4	4	1 Up
9	3	4	2 Up
10	6	5	1 Up
11	4	3	All Square
12	4	3	1 Down
13	4	5	All Square
14	3	5	1 Up
15	4	5	2 Up
16	3	4	3 Up

Matchplay is a golf format in which two players or two teams compete directly against each other on a hole-by-hole basis rather than the total number of shots in a round. This is how it works:

a. In match play, each hole is treated as a separate contest. The objective is to win as many holes as possible during a round. Each hole is either won, lost or drawn.

b. The player (or team) with the lowest score on each hole wins that hole. The player or team who wins a hole is said to be one up. If both players (or teams) score the same on a given hole, it is said to be halved.

c. If a player (or team) wins more holes than their opponent, they win the match.

d. If a player (or team) is ahead by more than the number of holes remaining, the match ends without finishing the round. This is because it would not be possible for the other player (or team) to catch up.

Matchplay Scoring:

The match would then be over with Player A winning by 3 & 2. The winning margin is three holes, but there are only two holes remaining, so Player B could not possibly catch up.

Matchplay tactics are very different to those adopted by players during stroke play tournaments, most notably that the number of shots taken for the round is irrelevant. As the game is decided on a hole-by-hole basis, as long as you take fewer shots than your opponent, it doesn't matter how many shots it takes to achieve it.

The other thing to note in match play is that when a player is losing, they will generally need to play more aggressively to catch up. There are a couple of other major differences:

• If a player is, for example, three holes up with three holes to play, they don't need to win any of the remaining holes to win; they just have to make sure they don't lose them all.

• Players don't have to complete each hole. If a player concedes a stroke – almost always a putt – to their opponent, the opponent picks up their ball, takes the score they would have made and moves on to the next hole. Similarly, if a player were to hit their ball into a lake twice and also into the woods, it would be obvious that they were going to lose the hole, so, to save time, they can concede the hole.

The Ryder Cup takes place over three days with three different formats:

1. Fourball
2. Foursomes
3. Singles

The first two days include four fourball matches and four foursome matches. The final day is reserved for twelve singles matches.

Fourballs

In Ryder Cup match play golf, the teams are divided into pairs with one pair from each team playing together at the same time. They each use their own ball, therefore there are four balls on each hole in play. To score, the team will take the lowest of their two players scores for the hole, and that will be their team score. A tie in the lowest scores results in the hole being halved.

Foursomes

In foursomes golf, each pair shares a ball, and players take turns hitting the team's ball until each hole is finished. The players hit alternative tee shots, with one starting on odd-numbered holes and the other hitting first on even-numbered holes. The team with the lowest score on each hole wins that hole. If their scores are tied, the hole is halved.

Singles

In singles, every player from each team competes in twelve head-to-head matches. The player with the lowest score on each hole wins that hole. If their scores are level, the hole is halved.

How Play Unfolds

On Friday morning, there are four matches with eight players from each team playing. This means that four from each team will miss this session. It is up to the captains to select the eight players who play, which is a crucial task. They need to assess personalities as well as an individual's form and experience. If a captain makes the right decision, it is possible for a 'lower ranked' pairing to beat higher-ranked opponents.

How do captains determine pairings in the Ryder Cup?

The pairings for Ryder Cup matches are anything but random. Once the teams of twelve have been confirmed, captains and their vice-captains will consider who to pair with whom based on chemistry, how one player's game complements that of another, who is playing well, and which format is being played. Sometimes they get it right, and sometimes they don't.

In 2004, US captain Hal Sutton got it spectacularly wrong. He chose Tiger Woods and Phil Mickelson (who were ranked one and two in the World) to play together. However, things didn't go to plan. When asked later by a journalist, Phil Mickelson stated that he and Tiger were only given two days' notice that they were to be paired, which gave them no time to prepare. At the time, Phil and Tiger were fierce rivals, and the perception behind the scenes was that Tiger didn't respect Phil or his game, which irritated Phil. When you bring that to a Ryder Cup pairing where any small niggle can cause a much bigger problem, you're asking for trouble and on this occasion, the problem was with the ball. At that time, in foursomes golf, both players had to play with the same ball, which was never going to work with Phil and Tiger, who used very different balls in their game. (This rule has since changed, and teams can now change the make of the ball on the tee of each hole).

Phil said, *"Tiger found out the year before when we played at the Presidents Cup in 2003 (also a match play tournament) that the golf ball I was playing with was not going to work for him. He plays a very high spin ball, and I play a very low spin ball, so we only had two days to come up with a solution. I grabbed a couple of dozen of his balls and tried to learn his golf ball in a few hours, trying to find out how far the ball goes. It forced me to stop my normal preparation for a tournament - to stop chipping and putting and sharpening my game - in an effort to learn a whole different golf ball. In the history of my career, I have never ball-tested two days prior to a major. Had we known a month in advance, we might have been able to make it work. I think we probably would have made it work."* Phil's final comment some twelve years later referenced the captain.

"It all starts with the captain," he said, *"that's the guy who has to bring twelve strong individuals together and bring out their best. That's the whole foundation of the team. I hear, well, you guys just need to play better or putt better. Absolutely, you do. But also, you play how you prepare."*

Ryder Cup Scoring

Each match is worth one point, with matches ending in a tie worth ½ point to each side. The first team to reach 14 ½ points (out of 28) wins the Ryder Cup. If the score ends in a 14-all tie, the team holding the Ryder Cup retains it.

There is one Ryder Cup story that I feel compelled to recount to you. It occurred back in 2012 near Chicago at the Medinah Country Club. The European team were being thrashed but had started a spirited recovery. It was on the Sunday afternoon and the singles competition was underway. Rory McIlroy, who was at the time ranked the best player in the world, was due to start his round at 12:12 Eastern Time, however, Medinah is in the Central Time Zone. Rory's real start time was therefore an hour earlier at 11:25. In the United States, everything runs on Eastern Time, which included the phone McIlroy was using and the television in his hotel room. The latter he was casually watching less than half an hour before his singles match was due to begin.

Suddenly, the European team realised that their top player was nowhere to be seen so they called him - and that's when the penny dropped. Usually, it takes 15 minutes to get from the hotel to the golf course, so with McIlroy still having half an hour until his tee time, he would have had plenty of time, however, on that particular day the traffic was gridlocked - due in no small part to the 40,000 spectators who had piled onto the course.

As luck would have it, the Deputy Chief of Police was able to drive McIlroy through the chaos enabling him to arrive at the course with ten minutes to spare. So, whilst he made it just in time, Rory was unable to warm up or do any practice shots. Nonetheless, he still won his match. If, though, he had been unable to secure the assistance of the Deputy Chief of Police and had arrived a couple of minute late for his tee time, then the first hole would have been forfeited. If he had been five minutes late, a point would have been given to the USA team which would have nullified the comeback efforts of the European team and they would have lost the Cup that year.

As it was, they won - just!

16. Interesting Golf Quotes

Ben Hogan

"The most important shot in golf is the next one."

Tom Watson

"Golf is a game of ego, but it's also a game of integrity: the most important thing is you do what is right when no one is looking."

Bobby Jones

"Golf is a game that is played on a five-inch course - the distance between your ears!"

Mark Twain (attributed)

"Golf is a good walk, spoiled."

Gary Player (won nine major championships!)

"The more I practice, the luckier I get."

Chapter Five

RUGBY UNION

"Rugby is a hooligans game played by gentlemen."

Winston Churchill

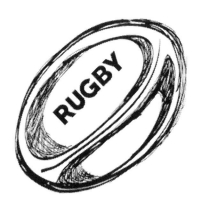

Note: Although there are two forms of Rugby - Rugby Union and Rugby League - I will be focusing on Rugby Union, which is the most popular form of the sport. There are, though, many similarities between the two forms.

Rugby is full of strange terms! Therefore, I have compiled a brief Glossary which you can refer back to as you continue through this chapter.

Glossary

- **Ball held up in goal**: When a player who is attempting to score a try, is held up in the in-goal area so that the player cannot ground the ball, the ball is dead. A five-metre scrum is formed. The attacking team gets the put in.

- **Binding/Bound**: When players are bound together as the starting point for a scrum.

- **Blind-side**: The narrower side of the pitch relative to the position of the set piece or breakdown. A rugby pitch is typically 70m wide, so if a scrum is awarded 10m from the right-hand touchline, that side of the pitch is known as the blind-side.

- **Box kick**: A type of kick carried out by a scrum half. It is made from the base of a ruck or maul and usually has the forwards in a position to protect the scrum half

- **Gate**: The gate is a space formed by imaginary lines that span the width of a tackled player. All players entering a breakdown or ruck must do so while 'coming through the gate'. Failure to do so will lead to a penalty.

- **Hands**: "Hands!" is a slang rugby term. It refers to hands in the ruck, which is punishable with a penalty.

- **Heeled (Back)**: A way of passing the ball to a teammate using your feet.

- **Knock-On**: When a player fails to catch a ball and spills it forward.

- **In Goal Area**: The area behind the posts.

- **Lineouts**: The way a game is resumed after the ball has left the side of the pitch.

- **Mauls**: When a player carrying the ball is held by one or more opponents and where one or more of the ball carrier's teammates bind (grab) onto the ball carrier.

- **Openside**: The larger side of the pitch. The opposite of the blind-side.

- **Out on the full**: When a player kicks the ball into touch, it will either have bounced first or not. If it goes into touch without bouncing, it is known as being kicked out 'on the full'.

- **Phase**: The period between breakdowns. You might see stats or hear commentators refer to the number of phases. This is a measure of continuity and measures a team's ability to retain possession.

- **Rucks**: This is a phase of play where one or more players from each team are in physical contact; crucially they are all on their feet.

- **Scrum**: The way the game resumes after a foul (more serious offences result in a penalty).

- **Turnover**: This occurs when a defender drives opponents back to gain possession.

CONTENTS

1. What is Rugby Union?

Rugby Union - also referred to as 'Rugby'- is a full-contact team sport that was first played in Rugby School (a public school in the United Kingdom where it was developed) during the first half of the 19th century. It is based on running with an oval-shaped ball in hand and is played on a rectangular field known as a pitch. As the game has evolved, World Rugby has determined that pitches must be between 94 and 100 metres long and 68 and 70 metres wide. More often than not,

ENGLAND v. SCOTLAND AT BLACKHEATH, 1901. FROM THE PICTURE BY ALLAN STEWART.

modern pitches are standardised at 100 metres by 68 metres. The game includes both collaboration with teammates and physical confrontation with the opposition. Each team comprises 15 players who fight to gain possession of the ball and pitch territory, with the aim of scoring points.

Rugby is undoubtedly one of the most physical games with its objective being to score more points than their opponents within the 80-minute time frame allotted. The team with the greater number of points at full-time is the winner. If both teams end on the same number of points, the match is a draw unless it is a knock-out match, which I will cover later.

During the game, the team in possession of the ball moves it up the pitch towards 'their opponent's end' through distinct 'phases of play'. Forward passes are not allowed, but players may run forward with the ball in hand or kick it forward for a chase. The opposing team's objective is to intercept the ball by tackling the player with the ball or catching a kicked ball. The idea is for them to regain control and begin moving the ball back the other way.

2. Equipment

- Rugby boots
- An oval-shaped rugby ball

- A team jersey
- A gum shield – to protect teeth
- A scrum cap – some players wear to protect their ears
- Two goalposts
- A kicking tee

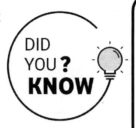

DID YOU **?** **KNOW**

Rugby balls were originally made from pig bladders, tightly stitched to trap air. The distinctive plum shape of a rugby ball makes it aerodynamic and, therefore, easier to hold and pass.

3. The History of Rugby

Though the origins of Rugby can be traced back to various forms of early university and school football, the most influential version was the one played at Rugby School in England. It is from here that modern-day rugby was effectively developed. According to legend, in 1823, Rugby School student William Webb Ellis picked up the ball during a standard game of football and ran with it. Though players cannot carry the ball within the rules of football, this incident gave rise to the evolution of Rugby, a sport in which players are allowed to carry the ball.

The game gained popularity throughout the 19th century, and in 1871, the governing body of the sport, the Rugby Football Union (RFU), was formed. The RFU standardised the rules, resulting in the development of distinctive *scrums* and *lineouts* to restart play.

During the early days of rugby, Richard Lindon (an inventor and leather shop owner) found his leather to be highly sought after for producing rugby balls. Due to the increased demand, Richard's wife, Rebecca, began assisting him in the manufacturing process, which sadly led to her untimely death. This was blamed on her ingesting germs from blowing up the pig bladders, a tragedy that prompted Lindon to search for an alternative material (Indian rubber) to use.

The game spread quickly beyond England, with the first international match taking place in Edinburgh in 1871 between Scotland and England, with Scotland winning 1-0. In 1875, Ireland began playing England and Scotland, and six years later, in 1881, Wales joined in. Two more years later, in 1883, the first international tournament began, which became known as the Home Nations Championship.

In 1895, the Rugby Football League (RFL) split from the Rugby Football Union (RFU), leading to the creation of the Rugby League (for the purposes of this book we are going to focus on Rugby Union). In 1910, France joined the Home Nations Championship leading it to it subsequently becoming known as the Five Nations (England, Scotland, Ireland, Wales and France). It wasn't until the year 2000, when Italy joined, that the championship became known as the Six Nations. Aside from the Five/Six Nations Championship, the inaugural Rugby World Cup took place in 1987 and was won by New Zealand, who had the advantage of being hosts. Today, Rugby Union is played all over the world, with particularly strong teams coming out of Australia, Zealand and South Africa.

Notable Dates:

1823 - During a game of football at Rugby School in England, William Webb Ellis picked up the ball and ran with it in his arms. The Rugby World Cup Trophy is now named after him.

1846 - The rules of rugby football were established by pupils from Rugby School.

1870 - Richard Lindon invented a rubber tube and pump. This 'standardised' the shape of the ball and this design remains close to what is used today.

1871 – The Calcutta Cup's first international match was won 1-0 by Scotland in Edinburgh against England.

Rugby Union was once an Olympic sport having been introduced to the Summer Olympics by Pierre de Coubertin who had previously refereed the first French International game. France, Germany and Great Britain entered teams with France winning the Gold medal by beating both opponents. Rugby actually drew the largest crowd at those games but despite this, was dropped in 1924. A shorter version of the game, Rugby Sevens, played with seven-a-side was re-introduced in 2016 at the Rio Olympics.

DID YOU**?** KNOW

1872 - William Webb Ellis died four years before he was named as Rugby's inventor.

1877 - The first fifteen-a-side rugby match was held between England and Ireland.

1894 - The scoring system was established.

1895 – Rugby split into two codes, Rugby Union and Rugby League, due to a disagreement over compensating players for lost work time, known as broken time. The split highlighted the social and class divisions of the sport in England. Those playing Rugby Union in the South of England remained largely amateur for a further 100 years.

1905 – A New Zealand team touring the British Isles performed a *haka*[1] before each match on the tour. In response, Welsh player Teddy Morgan led the crowd in singing the Welsh National Anthem. After Morgan began singing, the crowd joined in. This was the first time a national anthem was sung at the start of any sporting event.

1995 - Formal restrictions on payments to players in Rugby were lifted in 1995, making it an openly professional sport.

4. The World Rugby Core Values and Playing Charter

Rugby has a particular ethos that it has held onto over time. The game is not just played by following rules but also by upholding the spirit of those rules. By being disciplined, controlled, and showing mutual respect, players create a sense of fellowship and fairness that defines rugby as we know it today. In 2009, rugby member unions identified integrity, passion, solidarity, discipline and respect as the key defining characteristics of rugby. These values are now collectively known as the World Rugby Core Values and are included in the World Rugby Playing Charter. This document (the World Rugby Playing Charter) ensures that rugby maintains its unique character both on and off the field. The core values help participants understand what makes the game special.

5. The Game

Games are divided into two 40-minute halves, with an interval of no more than 15 minutes between them. The sides exchange ends of the pitch after the half-time break. The referee will toss a coin to determine which team starts the match. Each half of the match begins with a dropkick – a player literally drops the ball and kicks it into the air - from the centre of the halfway line. Players on the same team are not allowed to be in front of the player taking the kick until after the ball has been kicked.

---

1 https://bit.ly/3yrzp8W

Players on the opposing team must be at least ten metres from the ball when it is kicked. The ball must also travel a minimum of ten metres towards the opposition before hitting the ground. If the kick fails to make ten metres or goes straight into touch (out of the playing area), the opposing captain can choose the sanction (punishment) for the kicking team. They can ask for either a scrum on the halfway line (with their team putting the ball into the scrum, which is a distinct advantage) or ask for the original kick to be retaken. If they feel that their scrum is strong, they will probably choose a scrum.

Usually, the team that is kicking the ball will opt to kick it high and a long way into the opposition's half of the pitch. This allows their own players more time to try and catch

the ball before the other team does.

As I will explain later, there are three ways to score points in Rugby Union. After a team scores points, the match is restarted by the other team taking a drop kick on the halfway line.

If there is an injury to a player, or if the referee decides to stop the game for any other reason, he will call out "time off," which means that the clock stops. This prevents the need to add 'additional time' at the end of the game so both players and spectators will always know when it is the end of a half or a game (40 or 80 minutes). However, if the ball is in play when 40 or 80 minutes have elapsed, the game continues until the ball leaves the pitch. If the referee awards a penalty or free kick after 80 minutes and the ball is in play, the game will continue until the move has ended, thereby allowing the penalty to be taken.

If in knockout stages of Rugby competitions such as the World Cup, the game is tied after full time, two 10-minute periods of extra time are added (with an interval of five minutes in between). If the scores are still level after 100 minutes, a further 20 minutes of sudden death extra time is played. If the sudden death extra time period results in no scoring, a kicking competition is used to determine the winner. No match in the history of the Rugby World Cup has ever gone past 100 minutes and therefore into a sudden death extra time period, although this nearly happened in the 2003 World Cup Final, with England's Jonny Wilkinson kicking a drop goal with seconds to spare to win the game.

6. The Players and their Positions

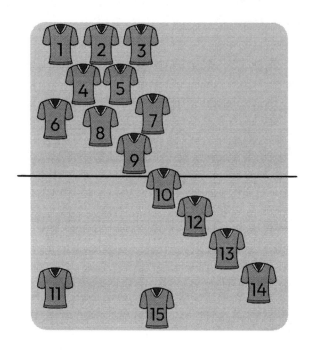

1. Loose-head Prop
2. Hooker
3. Tight-head Prop
4. Lock
5. Lock
6. Blindside Flanker
7. Openside Flanker
8. Number 8
9. Scrumhalf
10. Flyhalf
11. Winger
12. Inside Centre
13 Outside Centre
14. Winger
15. Fullback

As mentioned earlier, a rugby team consists of 15 players. Each one has a specific role and often a name which may or may not make immediate sense.

Rugby Union is known for being a sport that welcomes players of all shapes and sizes. Every position on the field demands a distinct combination of physical and technical abilities, which is what makes the sport so inclusive.

There are eight forwards (numbers one to eight) and seven backs (numbered nine to 15) These names are common for most positions but some regional variations also exist.

7. The Players and their Roles

• THE FORWARDS: THREE PARTS

The forwards' primary duties involve acquiring and maintaining possession of the ball. They also have a crucial role in tackling and rucking opposing players. These positions are typically filled by larger and stronger players who participate in the scrum and lineout.

When in scrum formation, they are commonly referred to as the 'pack'. There are three parts to the forwards as follows:

i.   Front row

The front row is made up of three players: two props (the loose-head prop and the tight-head prop) and the hooker. The main duty of the props is to assist the hooker in scrums, support the jumpers in lineouts, and provide strength and power in rucks and mauls.

Meanwhile, the hooker is a crucial position that plays a vital role in both attacking and defensive plays. They are responsible for winning the ball in scrums and typically throw the ball in at lineouts. The reason that the two props are referred to as loose-head and tight-head is that when they are in scrum formation, one of them will have opposition players on either side of them (the tight-head) and the other will have a player on only one side (the loose-head).

ii.   Second row

The second row is made up of two players who are also referred to as locks or lock forwards. These players are typically the tallest members of a team and are specialists in jumping during lineouts. Their primary responsibility is to make a standing jump with support from other forwards, in order to catch the ball or make sure that it lands on their team's side. Additionally, locks play a crucial role in the scrum by binding directly behind the three front-row players and contributing to the forward drive.

iii.   Back row

The back row, not to be confused with the 'backs', is the third and final row of the forwards. They are often referred to as the 'loose' forwards because they are not 'bound' to other players. The three positions in the back row are the two flankers and the Number 8. The two flankers are called the blind-side flanker and openside flanker because during scrums, one of them has most of the pitch to guard (openside), and the other (blind-side) has a smaller amount to defend (see later for more information). Their main role is to win possession through 'turnovers'. The Number 8 packs down between the two locks at the back of the scrum and their role here is to control the ball after it has been heeled back from the front of the pack by the hooker as well as linking between the forwards and backs during attacking phases.

•   THE BACKS: THREE PARTS

The role of the backs is to create and convert point-scoring opportunities. They are generally smaller, faster and more agile than the forwards. Another distinction between the backs and the forwards is that the backs are expected to have superior kicking and ball-handling skills, especially the fly-half, scrum-half and fullback.

i.   Half-backs

The half backs consist of two positions, the 'scrum-half' and the 'fly-half'. The scrum-half is the link between the forwards and the backs. They receive the ball from the lineout and remove the ball from the back of the scrum, usually passing it to the fly-half. They also feed the ball into the scrum. The fly-half is crucial to a team's game plan, orchestrating its performance. They are usually the first to receive the ball from the scrum-half following a breakdown, lineout or scrum and need to be decisive and effective at communicating with their outside backs. Many flyhalves are also their team's goal kickers.

ii.   Three-quarters

There are four three-quarter positions: two centres (inside and outside) and two wings (left and right). The centres will attempt to tackle attacking players when their team is defending and whilst in attack, they will employ speed and strength to breach opposition defences. The wings are generally positioned on the outside of the backline. Their primary function is to finish off moves and score tries. Wings are usually the fastest players in the team and are elusive runners who use their speed and guile to avoid tackles.

iii.   Full back

The fullback is normally positioned several metres behind the back line. Fullbacks often field opposition kicks and are usually the last line of defence should an opponent break through the defensive line. Two of the most important attributes of a good full-back are dependable catching skills and a good kicking game.

8. Playing the Game

Passing

A player may pass the ball to a teammate who is in a better position to continue an attack, but the ball must not go forward. By advancing with the ball and passing it backwards, teams can gain territory. If the ball is passed forward, the referee will stop the game and award a scrum to the opposing team.

Knock-on

If a player accidentally drops the ball or it bounces off their hand or arm and moves forward, it is called a knock-on. This results in the opposing team being awarded a scrum, causing the team who made the mistake to lose possession of the ball.

Kicking

If a player chooses not to pass or run with the ball, they can gain territory by kicking it forward. Any teammates that are in front of the ball when it is kicked are considered to be offside until they return behind the kicker. The player who kicks the ball or, crucially, any of their teammates who were behind them when they kicked the ball can run forward, and when they pass teammates, they put those teammates onside.

The downside of kicking the ball is that, more often than not, possession is given away so retaining possession of the ball following a kick is a challenge.

Kicking strategies include:

• Kicking into space so that teammates have time to catch it before an opponent reaches it.

• Kicking out wide, at an oblique angle, so that the winger or outside centre can catch the ball and run forward with it.

• Kicking the ball to touch (out of play), resulting in a lineout with the opposition having to throw in the ball. Though this concedes possession, it allows the kicking team to contest for the ball in a much more advantageous position on the pitch.

When a player kicks the ball into touch (out of play) four different outcomes are possible:

• If the ball bounces on the pitch first, the result is a line out to the opposition from where the ball crossed the touchline.

• If the ball is kicked directly into touch from within the kicker's own 22-metre line, the opposition takes a lineout at the point where the ball crosses the touchline.

• If the ball is kicked into touch directly by a player outside their 22-metre line, the lineout is formed where the kick was taken. This is a major mess up, and the player will not be popular with their teammates!

• A new rule was introduced in July 2022 to encourage attacking play. It is known as the 50:22 rule. If a player kicks the ball from their own half (the 50 part) and it lands in the opposing team's 22 (the 22 bit) and rolls into touch, the kicker's team will now get the throw in. This is a major change and has definitely encouraged attacking play. The reason why it has encouraged attacking play is that it forces the opposing wingers to defend further back, leaving more space for the attacking team.

9. Scoring Points

Unlike in football where there is only one way to score, in Rugby, there are four main ways to score points:

i)   A **try** which is worth **5 points**

A try is scored when the ball is grounded over the opponent's try line in the 'in-goal' area. The player must exert downward pressure on the ball whilst being in control of it, but not necessarily touching it. They cannot have any part of their body in touch. If there is any doubt, then the attacking team is awarded a five-metre scrum (meaning that their scrum-half puts the ball in). From May 2020, the goal posts and padding no longer counted as part of the goal line so scoring a try by grounding the ball at the foot of the posts, is now not allowed. If an attacking player is tackled short of the line but immediately reaches out and places the ball on or over the line, a try is awarded. This is not considered to be a 'double movement', much to the disappointment of the defending team.

The number of points awarded for a try was increased from one point in 1890 to two points in 1891 and then again to three in 1893. It stayed at three for the next 78 years until the value for a try was increased to four points in 1971. It was increased again 21 years later to the current five points in 1992.

Originally, points were not awarded for tries. If a team scored a try, it gave them the opportunity to TRY a kick at goal, hence its name. If successful, the kick would earn the team just one point, so all the hard work was done for no certain reward. The only time tries were considered was if a match ended with the same number of goals having been kicked by each side. The first international match between England and Scotland, for example, in 1871, ended with both sides having scored one goal. Scotland then won by virtue of having scored two tries, where England had only scored one.

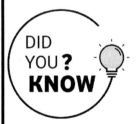
DID YOU**?** **KNOW**

ii)   A **conversion** which is worth **2 points**

After a try has been awarded, the goalkicker from the same team has the opportunity to 'convert' the try. To do this, they place the ball on the ground on the 22-metre line directly level with where the try was scored. They will try to kick the ball between the upright posts and over the crossbar. Often, the try scorer will aim to place the ball down under the posts to make the goalkicker's task easier. The goal kicker is now given 90 seconds to take the kick. You may notice that the two touch judges or linesmen will be behind the posts, and if the kick is successful, they will raise their flags.

iii)   A **drop goal** which is worth **3 points**

Any player can, at any point in the game and from any part of the pitch, attempt a drop goal. To do so, they must first drop the ball onto the ground and then kick it between the upright posts and over the crossbar. Incidentally between 1891 and 1948, drop goals were worth four points.

iv)   A **penalty** which is worth **3 points**

Over the course of a match, penalties usually produce the most points for a team. When a team is awarded a penalty, their captain may choose to kick at goal. The kicker must take the kick from the spot of the offence and within 60 seconds of the captain indicating their intention to do so. The team's captain has other options besides asking their kicker to attempt to score three points. More of this later. Incidentally, penalties were only worth two points before 1891.

As there are so many ways for points to be scored, here's an example of how two team's scores could accumulate:

Team A - Two tries and one conversion = (2 x 5) + 2 = 12 points
Team B – One try and two penalties = 5 + (2 x 3) = 11 points

In this match, Team A is currently ahead by 1 point.

When watching a game on TV, in the top corner (usually), you will see the score. For example, in the game above, the score would be shown as Team A - 12 ~ Team B - 11.

Usually the team mentioned first will be the Home team and the second one will be the Visitors. This does not apply in tournaments like the World Cup. Often, the broadcasters will also show the flags of the two competing teams beside their score.

10. Rules and Customs

Like many sports, Rugby Union is constantly evolving with new rules introduced pretty much every season. Generally, these rule changes are aimed at improving player safety, speeding up the game and enhancing the spectator experience. One of the most noticeable additional rules was introduced in 2023 and is known as the 'shot clock'. The idea was to reduce time-wasting within the game and determined that:

- A conversion must be taken within 90 seconds from when the try was awarded.
- A penalty kicker has 60 seconds to take a penalty kick.
- Teams must form a scrum within 30 seconds of the signal from the referee.

General Rules:

- Each team consists of 15 players and eight replacements.
- No shoulder pads are allowed.
- Every player on the Rugby pitch is allowed to run with the ball and tackle opponents.
- When a scrum is formed, the forwards and backs will get into their set positions which is why this is known as a 'set piece'.
- When a player is tackled, they have one second to let go of the ball. A player cannot touch it again until they are back standing on their own feet.
- When a player tackles an opponent, they can't pick up the ball until they are on their feet. This is one of the most common offences that leads to penalties. They must be standing to pick up the ball, and they cannot dive onto a loose ball.
- When a player is defending and a tackled player is on the ground, they must make sure they are on their side of the scrummage line before having any physical contact with the other team. Otherwise, they are offside. This happens when a defensive player is chasing a player from behind. The defensive player must run around the ruck and enter from the other side.

- In rugby, a 'phase' refers to the period of play between breakdowns. To illustrate, the first phase involves gaining possession of the ball during a lineout and passing it to a teammate who is then tackled. The second phase involves regaining possession of the ball after the ensuing breakdown and launching another attack. There is no limit (unlike in Rugby League) to the number of phases that can be played.

- If a team wins possession from an opposition scrum (i.e. the opposition scrum-half puts the ball in) it is known as winning one 'against the head'.

11. Team Tactics

For all its many complexities, rugby remains a simple game in essence. Points can be scored when a player is put into space and when an attacking team outnumbers those in defence. As such, rugby's holy grail lies in the creation of space. There are many tactics geared towards this, but primarily, it's about winning the ball quickly to move play away from opposition players. At the same time the team needs to inject pace and creativity in attack to make space for their player to score.

Developing tactics requires a thorough understanding of a team's strengths. You may, for example, have a team with a stronger group of forwards whilst another team may have a more agile and pacey group of back. It is also important to be aware of the team and individuals you're playing against and the tactics that they are likely to employ.

Using the physical strength of the forwards in scrums and rolling mauls can result in significant territorial gain. Forwards can 'pickup and drive' (gather the ball and take it forward with the support of teammates) until the moment is right to release it to their backs.

Each time a team gains possession, it will aim to move the ball forward towards the opposition's try line. An imaginary line is drawn across the pitch which is known as the 'gain line'. This line helps teams to determine whether or not they have made any territorial gain whilst in possession of the ball. As mentioned elsewhere, the ball has to be passed backwards but players can run forward with it.

Options for the captain when their team is awarded a penalty:

When the referee awards a penalty, the captain of the penalised team has to choose between the following two options:

1. Ask the 'goalkicker' (usually the fly-half, but not always) to attempt to kick the ball between the uprights and above the crossbar. If this is successful their team are awarded three points.

2. Ask the goalkicker to kick the ball 'directly' into touch. If they do this successfully (which they usually do) their team will be rewarded with the throw in at the lineout from where the ball crosses the line. This usually means they secure possession much further up the pitch. The benefit of this option is that they have an opportunity to score a try which is worth more points than a penalty

So, what criteria should a captain consider when deciding between these two very different options:

- Whether their team are winning or losing and by how much.
- The likelihood of their kicker succeeding with Option 1.
- The time left in the match.

Scenario 1

Their team are two points behind, with five minutes remaining and the kick is straightforward – probably choose Option 1.

Scenario 2

Their team are four points behind and there are eight minutes remaining and the kick is near the halfway line – they may believe that the kick is out of the range of their goalkicker – so they will probably choose Option 2 in the hope that their team can score a try from the resulting lineout which will hopefully take place near the opponents try line.

12. Set Pieces

Scrums

A scrum is used to restart play after minor infringements or when the ball is unplayable in a ruck or maul. At the scrum, all the forwards and the scrum halves are concentrated in one area on the pitch. This leaves space for the backs to mount an attack. A scrum (as defined by Wikipedia[1]) is:

1   https://bit.ly/3yjqwOD

"In rugby union a scrum is a means of restarting play after a minor infringement. It involves up to eight players from each team, known as the pack or forward pack, binding together in three rows and interlocking with the three opposing teams front row."

In theory, the ball is thrown into the middle of the tunnel between the two front rows so that the two hookers can compete it, attempting to hook it back in the direction of their teammates. In reality, however, the ball is not put in between the two front rows. The scrum-half instead places the ball to their own hooker and the referees turn a blind eye. Once possession has been secured by the hooker 'hooking' the ball to the back of the scrum, the scrum-half can either pass it to their backs or kick it into space.

Safety at the scrums

In the past, many rugby forwards experienced severe neck injuries, often caused by scrums. To address this issue, the International Rugby Board funded a research project worth £500,000 that was conducted by Bath University. The study revealed that while scrum-related injuries accounted for less than 10% of all playing injuries, they made up 40% of the most serious ones. The researchers found that the collision that occurred during the engagement phase was the primary cause of these injuries – something that was already known to the rugby community. The study also tested various referee scrum calls to determine the safest approach. The current approach (since 2013) is for the referees to use the following commands:

"Crouch, Bind, Set"

1. 'Crouch' tells the forwards to drop into a low position
2. 'Bind' tells the props to grip their opponent's jersey
3. 'Set' tells the players to engage and compete

Lineouts

The lineout is a means of restarting play after the ball has gone into touch. It usually involves all the forwards, leaving the rest of the pitch for the backs to plan an attack.

The team with the throw-in can choose a reduced number of players in a line out if they feel it is to their benefit. The key for the forwards is to win possession and distribute the ball effectively to their backs.

The forwards assemble in two lines, perpendicular to the touchline, one metre apart. The hooker throws the ball down the corridor between these two lines of players. They will liaise with their leader of the lineout to decide whether to aim at the front, the middle or the back of the lineout. Because the thrower's teammates know where the ball is likely to go, that team has an advantage in retaining possession. However, with speed of thought and movement, the opposition can compete for the ball, and the lineout sometimes results in a turnover of possession. The sanction for failing to throw the ball in straight is that the opposition can choose either a scrum or a lineout with their team throwing the ball in.

Lineout support

To allow players to catch high throws in the lineout, the catcher is now allowed to be lifted (since 1999) by team mates while jumping to catch the ball. Before this, lifting was not permitted. As safety is a prime concern, any player who is off the ground must be supported until that player returns to the ground. A player may not be tackled whilst in the air, and holding, shoving or levering on an opponent are all offences punishable with a penalty kick.

13. Tackle, Mauls and Rucks

As well as being an evasion game which requires the creation and use of space, rugby is also very much a contact sport. In fact, contact situations can be the very mechanism by which players create the space they need to attack.

The three most common contact situations which occur in open play are the **tackle**, the **ruck** and the **maul**.

The Tackle

A player may tackle an opposing player who has the ball by holding them and bringing them to the ground. Players can take hold of the ball carrier anywhere on their body except for their neck and head. Players cannot be touched whilst in the air. Breaking these rules could lead to a yellow or red card and certainly to a penalty.

To maintain the continuity of the game, the ball carrier must release the ball as soon as they are tackled. Also, the tackler must immediately release the ball carrier. Both players must roll away from the ball, which allows other players to compete for it, thereby starting a new phase of play. The failure of either player to do so will lead to a penalty.

Mauls

A maul occurs when a ball carrier is held by one or more opponents, and one or more of the ball carrier's teammates holds on (binds). All the players are on their feet, and the ball must be off the ground. A maul, therefore, needs a minimum of three players. The team in possession of the ball can attempt to gain territory by driving their opponents towards their opponents' goal line. The ball can then be passed backwards between players within the maul and eventually passed to a player who is not in the maul, or a player can leave the maul carrying the ball to run with it.

Rucks

If the ball is on the ground and players from both teams are 'on their feet' surrounding it, a ruck is formed. During a ruck, players are only allowed to use their feet to move the ball or push it towards their team's hindmost foot, where it can then be picked up. Players are not allowed to use their hands in the ruck, and doing so will result in a penalty for the opposing team.

Understanding the difference between a ruck and a maul can be difficult for both rugby players and spectators but here is a straightforward explanation that should help:-

- During a **ruck**, the ball is on the ground
- In a **maul**, it is typically held by a player

The advantage of a maul is that the ball carrier can keep moving forwards with the support of the pack. However, if the maul stops moving, the referee will give the team in possession a chance to 'move it or use it', and then usually a second chance 'use it or lose it'. If they fail to listen, the referee will award a scrum to the other side.

14. Breakdowns

The breakdown in rugby is the phase of play immediately after a tackle, where players attempt to gain possession of the ball. The breakdown has developed into the most important competition for possession of the ball.

Given that the first and most important principle of rugby is the contest for possession, it's unsurprising that there can be an average of 180 breakdowns in an average game of rugby. This equates to an astonishing figure of over two breakdowns per minute. The team in possession of the ball will, 94% of the time, hold onto possession following its breakdowns. Winning possession at breakdowns is known as winning a turnover. There are usually about ten of these turnovers in a match.

Turnovers are highly valued because they can convert defensive play into attacking play in a matter of seconds, which often changes the entire outcome of a game. Many tries, especially at international level, are scored from turnovers. The reason being that the defence is caught out of position. Once possession is lost, the attacking team will now be on the defence and must swiftly readjust its formation. It is this need to readjust that often leads to opportunities for scoring (by the opposing team) due to gaps which emerge on the field.

There are various techniques employed to gain possession of the ball via turnovers. The most commonly used include stripping the ball during a tackle, jackaling for the ball on the ground, and counter rucking at the breakdown.

a)   Stripping the ball

After a tackler releases the ball carrier, they will try to steal the ball.

b)   The jackal

Defenders can also steal the ball on the ground. They need to stay on their feet and cannot support their weight on an opposition player or go to ground. They must take their hands off the ball once a ruck is formed.

c)   Counter rucking

When teams counter ruck they compete for the ball on the ground so that the ball ends up on their side of the ruck.

Key points on turnovers

- Good defensive teams turn the ball over quickly rather than making lots of tackles.
- When ball carriers are tackled and they don't have support players to secure possession, defenders will jackal for the ball on the ground.

15. Offside

The offside Law in Rugby, much like in football, can be difficult to understand. Essentially, a player is considered offside if they are in front of the teammate who currently has possession of the ball or the teammate who last played the ball. Being offside is not an offence in itself, but the player cannot participate in the game until they are back onside. If they do, they will be penalised, and the opposition will be awarded a penalty.

When a player is on their feet and over the ball, which is on the ground during a tackle or ruck situation, offside lines are established. The offside line runs parallel to the goal line and is determined by the hindmost player in the tackle or on their feet over the ball. Is there more than one offside line?

16. Key Offences and the Punishments Awarded for Committing them!

Why did the whistle blow?

For anyone who is not familiar with the finer points of the Laws of rugby it can sometimes be hard to tell why the referee has stopped play for an infringement. Here I will go through some of the most common reasons why the whistle may have blown.

Basically, there are two categories of offence – signalled by the referee pointing their hand towards the non-offending team.

i. Less serious offences resulting in a scrum – referee's hand is horizontal to the ground:

- An accidental knock-on or a forward pass.

- A line out throw that isn't straight. The defending team takes the ball into their own 'in goal' area and either touches it down or puts it out of play within the 'in goal' area. This leads to the attacking team winning a scrum on the five-metre line.

- An attacking player carries the ball into the opposing teams' 'in goal area', but the defending team holds them up and prevents them from grounding the ball so no try is scored. The attacking team get a scrum on the five-metre line.

- If the ball is stuck in a ruck or maul, neither team is moving forward, and the ball can't be extracted, then the attacking team is awarded a scrum.

- A team has too many players in a lineout which awards a scrum to the other team.

- A team that has been awarded a penalty can opt for a scrum instead. They usually do this if they are dominant in the scrum but not doing so well with their kicking or with lineouts.

ii. **More serious offences resulting in the opposition being awarded a penalty. This means they can have a 'shot at goal' which if successful gives them three points. In this case the referee points his hand almost vertically. This is to distinguish from the less severe infringements:**

- Failing to release the ball after being tackled or failing to release the tackled player when tackling.

- Entering a ruck or maul from the side and not from the rear.

- Using hands to grab the ball in a ruck.

- Deliberately collapsing a scrum or maul.

- Failing to bind in a scrum.

- Being offside and not making an effort to move back onside.

- A high tackle (where contact is made above the shoulders).

- Tackling a player in the air or tackling a player who does not have the ball.

- Violent or foul play: punching, elbowing, kicking, head-butting, tripping etc.

- Not retreating ten metres away at a penalty.

A referee may choose to allow play to continue following an offence the penalised team have a good chance of scoring a try. The referee will announce 'advantage'. If a try is

177

scored it will stand (be allowed). The 'advantage' Law allows the game to flow with fewer stoppages and can last for several minutes. If the referee does not feel that the attacking team is likely to score, they will indicate the advantage to be over and the penalty is awarded where the original offence took place.

17. Player Sanctions

Cards are shown to any player who engages in foul play such as obstruction, unfair or dangerous play. A referee can show a yellow card to a player for any of these offences which means that the player has to leave the pitch (and cannot be replaced) for ten minutes. This is euphemistically known as being sent to the sin bin. If you are watching on TV, you may notice a small yellow card next to the team (who now only has 14 players) with a timer showing how long until the player can return to the field of play. For more serious offences, a referee can show a player a red card which means that they leave the pitch immediately. They cannot return or be replaced for the remainder of the match. Understandably, this can have a huge impact on the game.

The SAME whistle is used to start each World Cup. Gil Evans, a Welsh referee, used the same whistle for 20 years before donating it to the New Zealand Rugby Museum in 1969. The tradition of using this whistle was revived for the 1987 Rugby World Cup and has been continued for every tournament since. It is perhaps best not to think about the hygiene of this 100-year-old whistle!

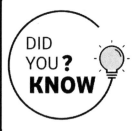

DID YOU? KNOW

The Bunker

This was introduced recently so that decisions as to whether an offence should merit a yellow or red card can be taken whilst play continues. The referee will cross their hands to indicate that a player should receive 'at least' a yellow card. The player then leaves the pitch and enters the bunker (sin bin) allowing play to continue. Specialists then review the incident whilst the game is still flowing and determine whether the player should receive a yellow or red card for their infringement. Once a decision has been made, the referee is informed as are both team captains and the appropriate action is then taken.

18. The Main Tournaments

The Rugby World Cup

This takes place every four years and is the pinnacle of the sport for every rugby union player. It began in 1987 when it was co-hosted by Australia and New Zealand. The final took place between New Zealand and France at Eden Park in Auckland in front of a capacity crowd of 48,035 who watched the hosts win. There were 16 countries involved in this first world cup.

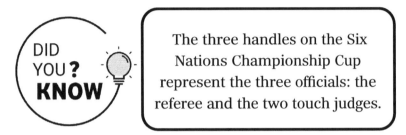

The three handles on the Six Nations Championship Cup represent the three officials: the referee and the two touch judges.

The most recent tournament (2023) was held in France with 20 teams taking part. This will rise to 24 teams in 2027. The 2023 Final was played in Paris in front of 80,065 fans who watched South Africa beat New Zealand.

In 2019, Japan made history as the first Asian country to reach the quarter finals of the Rugby World Cup – which they were also hosting. This achievement demonstrated that expanding rugby to new nations is a promising strategy to increase the sport's popularity.

Six Nations

This takes place annually between England, France, Ireland, Italy, Scotland and Wales. The matches are played in February and March with each team playing each other once. This means that every team plays five matches; two or three of these will be played 'at home' and they will travel for the remainder. Which games are played where alternates annually, meaning that if, for example, France play Ireland in Paris, the following year the same match will be played in Dublin.

Teams compete to win the Six Nations Championship Trophy, and aim to avoid finishing in last place, as this results in being awarded the Wooden Spoon. Since the Six Nations tournament began in 2000, England and Ireland are the only teams that have managed to avoid ever finishing last.

The Grand Slam and the Triple Crown

When a team wins every game in the Six Nations, they win the 'Grand Slam'. There is also the chance for England, Ireland, Scotland or Wales to win the Triple Crown which is awarded to one of these teams if they win all three of their matches against the other nations. The Triple Crown Tournament has been around since the original Home Nations Championship (which became the Six Nations) but the physical Triple Crown Trophy was only introduced in 2006.

There is also another special cup which is played between Scotland and England. It is known as the Calcutta Cup and is the oldest rivalry in rugby.

During British Colonial Rule, many soldiers were stationed in Calcutta and they, along with several other soldiers, formed the now defunct Calcutta Rugby Football Club in 1873. The formation of this club followed a match that had been played on

The nickname of the New Zealand Rugby Team is the All Blacks. This is because their kit is 'all black'.

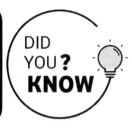

DID YOU **?** **KNOW**

Christmas Day in 1872 between 20 English and 20 Scottish soldiers. The Calcutta Rugby Football Club only existed for four years though, due to the rise in popularity of the sport of polo, and the departure of many of the original club founders. Its then honorary secretary and treasurer, GA James Rothney, wanted to do some 'lasting good' for the 'cause of rugby football' so he donated the remaining club funds of 270 Indian rupees (approximately £59 today) to the game. These coins were melted down by Indian silversmiths in 1878 to create an ornate trophy which has ever since been known as the Calcutta Cup. Due to its origins, this cup will only ever be contested by England and Scotland. The first official Calcutta Cup clash took place in Edinburgh in 1879 and resulted in a draw.

Where are the Six Nations matches played?

As of the 2024 competition, the Six Nations matches are held in the following stadia:

- Aviva Stadium in Dublin ~ capacity 51,700
- Murryfield Stadium in Edinburgh ~ capacity 67,144
- Principality Stadium in Cardiff ~ capacity 73,931

- Stade de France in Paris ~ capacity 81,338
- Stadio Olympico in Rome ~ capacity 72,698
- Twickenham Stadium in London ~ capacity 82,000

The Rugby Championship

This is an international tournament played between Argentina, Australia, New Zealand, and South Africa. Each team plays the others both home and away every year which means there are 12 matches in all. However, in Rugby World Cup years, the number of matches is halved, with each team only playing each other once. This is done to allow the teams more time to prepare for the Rugby World Cup.

19. New Zealand and The Haka

They are famous for their unmatched international success and have often been regarded as the most successful sports team in human history. From 1903 when they played their first game, to 2021, when they played their 612th, they won 77% of their matches. That statistic is absolutely crazy when you think about it. They were also the first rugby team to win 500 matches, one of many records establishing them as the world's best team.

There have been ten Rugby World Cups so far. New Zealand have won three, South Africa four, Australia have two, with England being the only team in the northern hemisphere to have won it at all, and then only once.

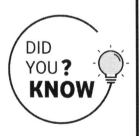

In the dim and distant past, rugby games did not have referees. Instead, the team captains would agree on the rules before the game and work together during the match to make decisions. The Rugby Union's 'advantage' Law was born from this practice since a team's Captain would not speak up or stop play if their team benefited from the other team's mistake.

The Haka (meaning dance in Māori) is a traditional dance of the Māori people and was first performed by the New Zealand Rugby Team, The Natives, in 1888 to demonstrate their pride, strength and unity. It has been performed before games ever since and has become a symbol of rugby for New Zealand. Whether you're a Kiwi or not, it's one of those spine-tingling moments when you know a big game is about to be played. Although the New Zealanders are the most famous exponents of the Haka, it is also performed by other Pacific countries such as Samoa, Fiji and Tonga.

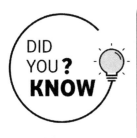

DID YOU ? KNOW

The only player who is allowed to talk to the referee is the Captain. You will notice that when the Captain addresses the Ref, he will often call him Sir.

Prior to New Zealand legend Wayne 'Buck' Shelford taking the helm in the mid-1980s and making his team actually practice the haka, it was more of a novelty for supporters and only performed at away matches, often rather shambolically. That's all changed now. The *wana* (passion or intensity) with which a haka is performed runs high in the team, and the blood-curdling roar has become one of the most loved sporting traditions in the world. Sometimes, though, the response to the New Zealand haka from their opposition is not always favourable. Whilst some teams stand by and grin wryly, others have walked straight up to the All Blacks and looked them in the eye with one side even responding with their own war dance. Maybe the English should try their own version with Morris dancers!

What is the most effective way to react, though? After all,, being too aggressive might fire up the All Blacks even more, so it could backfire.

At the World Cup in 1987, the French threw one of their most intimidating players right into the mix. Sebastien Chabal, known as the Caveman, stared into the souls of the Kiwis and certainly looked up for the challenge whilst the rest of the French team stood a few feet away.

Years later, in 2007, during the quarter final of the World Cup, a star-studded New Zealand team performed the haka to the French players at the Millennium Stadium in Cardiff. When France went on to win the match, their victory was considered that much sweeter having been a nation to 'take on' the New Zealand haka in the past.

20. Match Officials

The match is under the control of a referee, two assistant referees and a television match official or TMO.

The Referee (or simply The Ref or Sir!)

The referee organises the coin toss with the captains prior to the match to decide who kicks off first. During the match itself, the referee is the sole judge of fact and of Law. It is essential that all players respect the referee's decisions at all times.

The Referee and Communication

Rugby is unique in the way that the referee communicates with players and the wider public. Firstly, before the game begins, referees will call in the coaches and captains to explain how they intend to referee the match. They will discuss what they consider to be the key issues. This is because a lot of decisions are based on how the referee 'interprets' rules.

During the game, they will explain to the captain (and only the captain) the rationale for their interpretation of the laws. Sometimes, they will say to the captain, *"I have warned you before, go talk to your players; if this offence happens again, I will act."*

When he was England Coach, Sir Clive Woodward employed the world's leading visual awareness coach, Sherylle Calder. He wanted to find out if his players were using space efficiently. The idea was to try to determine where the next passage of play was likely to be. It was part of his strategy to get the 'extra one per cent'.

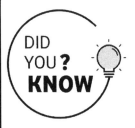

The referee will also be 'miked up' so that anyone can hear what is being said to the players. This is key to helping those watching in the stadium (and professional commentators) understand why decisions have been made.

Assistant Referees

There are two assistant referees, (also known as linesmen) one on either side of the pitch. Their role is to assist the referee in many ways such as when (and where) the ball crosses the line for a lineout and whether a penalty kick is successful or not. They can also alert the referee if they see anything the referee may have missed.

Television Match Official (TMO)

Often referred to as the TMO, a television match official may be appointed to assist the referee in decision-making. They can only rule on exactly what the referee asks to be reviewed, such as whether a try was scored or if a pass was forward. However, the TMO can direct the referees' attention to foul play by speaking to him through their earpiece. Television match officials are commonly used in first-class and international televised games.

Where match officials believe that an infringement may have occurred in the build up to a try being scored, they can use technology to help with their decision. However, unlike in Football, they can only go back two phases of play, so if an offence occurred earlier than this, then they have to ignore it.

21. The Coach

The role of the coach varies greatly depending on the level at which the team operates. At international level the coach is responsible for team selection, tactics, motivation, performance and results. Often teams will have specialist assistants looking after the scrum, the backs and the lineout.

A head coach will approach problems by considering all the coaching disciplines. This means thinking about the psychological, medical and physical as well as normal rugby skills, strategy and tactics. The role of the head coach is to review all these areas with the specialists and then support and challenge. The coach will have access to a medical support team, fitness advisers and other sports science support.

Replacements

As well as the 15 players in the starting line-up, a team will also have eight replacements (known as substitutes in football). Hence, you may hear the phrase that Rugby is now a 23-player team.

The coach will choose the replacements and has to make a tactical decision as to how many of the eight should be forwards or backs. If a player is injured, but the injury may not be too serious, they can be 'temporarily' replaced whilst the injury is assessed. You may have heard the expression 'blood replacement'. This is when a player bleeds, but it is not immediately clear how serious the injury is.

It is quite common for teams to decide when to replace certain players at specific times. For example, the coach may decide to change the entire front row after 60 minutes. This has the advantage that the initial three players in the front row know that they are not playing the whole game and can play accordingly.

Up until 2016, the number of replacements was limited to three. All replacements, whatever the reason, counted towards the limit during a match but in 2016, World Rugby changed the law so that replacements made for a player deemed unable to continue (due to foul play) would no longer count towards the three-replacement match limit.

History of Replacements

In 1924, New Zealand suggested that replacing injured players should be permitted. This idea was turned down. They tried again in 1932, 1947 and in 1952 without success. It seemed that if you had an injury, you simply got on with it. Either that or injured players left the pitch reducing the overall number remaining on their team.

In 1966, England played France and, during this match, the English captain, David Perry, suffered an injury. He elected to play on. It subsequently became apparent that his decision to remain on the pitch had exacerbated an existing knee injury, leading to the end of his career. This incident further increased calls for injury replacements to be permitted, but it still took a further two years until the rules were changed in 1968. Even then a Doctor was required to certify a player as unfit to continue and teams were only allowed a maximum of two replacements. Tactical replacements were eventually permitted too, but not until much later on in 1996.

22. Eligibility to Play International Rugby

To many this has become a contentious issue when players on the international stage are seen playing for a country which is not of their birth. I thought it might be helpful to therefore clarify the eligibility rules.

There are four ways a player can be eligible to represent a country at international level:

1. They were born in the country.

2. They have a parent or grandparent who was born in the country. Adoptive parents count.

3. They have lived in the country for 60 consecutive months to qualify on residency. This was increased on 1 January 2017 from 36.

4. They have completed ten years of cumulative residence in the country before playing.

With regards to **point three**, players who moved countries before 31 December 2017 will be eligible under the three-year rule. Anyone who moved after 1 January 2021 will be subject to the new five-year rule.

When is a player 'captured' by a country?

Captured is the term used when a player becomes tied to one country and can no longer represent another nation on the international stage. This happens when a player plays for one of three teams:

1. The **first 15-a-side** national team.

2. The senior sevens team of a country where the player is aged 20 or older or, if at an Olympics or Sevens World Cup, the player has reached the age of majority 18.

The **second 15-a-side** national team. This is where it gets slightly complicated because each country has different classifications for their second team. It could be an A team, like England Saxons, but it's up to each country to decide which team they want to designate as their 'second' team.

23. Fun Facts

1. The 1995 film '*Invictus*' was inspired by the sport of rugby. It illustrates how the then South African President, Nelson Mandela, used their rugby team as a way to unite the country. Other films such as '*Forever Strong*' and '*Murderball*' have also been inspired by the game of rugby.

2. Players can be known as much for their hairstyles as their sporting prowess. It is not uncommon for them to have long hair or even have designs shaved into their hairstyle. A style known as 'rugby hair', is often used to describe these unique and unusual looks.

3. Singing is synonymous with rugby. Both teams will often join in a song before and after the game along with spectators who will raise the roof throughout. This is believed to promote sportsmanship within the game and between teams.

(Facts adapted from a blog post featured on rugbynation.com on the 10th March 2023, 10 Rugby Facts You May Not Have Known.)

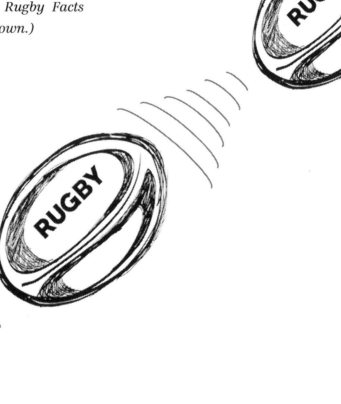

Chapter Six

TOUR de FRANCE

"To say that the race is a metaphor for life is to miss the point. The race is everything. It obliterates whatever isn't racing. Life is the metaphor for the race."

Donald Antrim

CONTENTS

1. What is the Tour de France?

The Tour de France is a bike race which runs over a period of 23 days in July, primarily in France. There are 21 'stages' (i.e. one per day) and two well-deserved rest days. The riders pass through many parts of France, including the Pyrenees and the Alps, and finish on the Champs-Elysees in Paris. The main competition is known as the 'General Classification' or GC for short. There are other awards given to various riders, such as best young rider, and those that win each individual stage.

Tour de France c.1930

2. Objectives

The objective is to finish all 21 stages faster than anyone else. The entire course covers over 3,500 kilometres, with the riders negotiating serious mountains as well as flat sprints. Each rider forms part of a team of eight who work together to win the coveted prize.

As well as the Tour de France, similar competitions take place in Spain and Italy which compete with the Tour de France for publicity, 'box office' competitors and funding. It often frustrates the Italians when top riders use the Giro (Italian major tour) as a practice run for the Tour de France, which takes place just a few weeks later.

Some specialist sprint riders will also aim for early 'stage' wins and then drop out of the race when they reach the mountains. Understandably, this is frustrating for enthusiasts (and other competitors) as they see this as not playing by the spirit of the competition. However, the riders who do this are happy to declare they have 'done the job' and 'won a stage' of the Tour de France.

Each team will have a team leader who will usually excel in all disciplines, such as time trials and climbing mountains, as well as having exceptional endurance. The rest of the team will act as his supporters (known as *domestiques*, which is French for helper).

Domestiques are chosen for the different strengths they have which will help the leader to win. It is not uncommon for one of these 'helpers' to become a team leader in future years.

3. Equipment

<u>For the rider</u>

- A lightweight carbon fibre bike weighing no more than 6.8 kg, which is roughly the weight of a vacuum cleaner or a brick
- Specially designed bike shoes known as cleats
- A bike helmet
- Gloves
- Nutrition.
- A water bottle
- A pair of sunglasses – the race takes place in July
- A means to communicate with their team

One thing riders don't carry is a puncture repair kit. This is because the team provides spare wheels; however this wasn't always the case. Riders used to have to mend their own punctures which would have a more detrimental effect on their race than it does today.

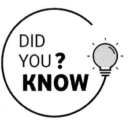
DID YOU **?** KNOW

<u>A typical team consists of:</u>

- Eight riders

- A coach

- Four mechanics

- A cook

- A technical director

- A doctor

- A photographer

- Ten vehicles (including various support vehicles)

- A truck (for breakdowns or repairs)

- 27 road bikes

- 18 time trial bikes

- 80 pairs of wheels

- 2,000 water bottles

- 400 musettes – like lunch boxes

4. The History

The Tour de France was created in 1903 by two Frenchmen: Henri Desgrange, who was the editor of L'Auto, and George Lefevre, a rugby and cycling reporter. The primary aim was to publicise and improve the circulation of the sports paper. When it was launched, the Tour consisted of just six stages, reaching a total of 2,428 km. This meant that riders needed to complete over 400km per day (stage), so they had to ride day and night! They also had to carry out their own repairs and mend their own punctures. In contrast, today, if a rider gets a puncture, then the 'team' simply replace the wheel or, if needed, the entire bike.

There were 20,000 curious spectators lining the streets of Paris for the first event, which ended up being so popular that the circulation of the paper quadrupled. Though this was a resounding success, the second Tour de France the following year almost ended up being the last. Many of the riders blatantly cheated by catching trains and even sabotaging each other's bikes. Some riders spread nails and broken glass over the road and were known to spike each other's drinks the night before.

In order to avoid the Tour descending into chaos, the organisers realised that they would have to introduce some actual rules. Over the next few years, rides into the Pyrenees and Alps were added which increased the overall race distance, however each stage (average) length was then shortened. The net result was an extension of the Tour's duration to 23 days which allowed for more rest and recovery periods for the riders.

There are usually 22 teams of eight riders competing in the Tour, and they literally do everything together: race, eat, recover, and repeat. Most stages last approximately five hours. Each team is (financially) sponsored, typically by banks, energy companies, and bicycle companies.

The average cost of a Tour de France bike is between £10,000 and £15,000! Also, riders use the same tyres throughout a stage, regardless of the weather. There is no such thing as a wet-weather tyre. Riders do, however, use different bikes for the various stages depending on the terrain. Disc wheels, for example, are more efficient during the flat sprint stages but are less stable in the mountain regions.

Many people are under the impression that cyclists complete the Tour as individuals - which is technically correct; after all, there can only be one winner – but it is very much a team sport. The race leader wears a bright yellow jersey (more of this later), which can be seen from helicopters (to help television coverage), and after each stage, he will stand on a podium (as the stage winner), which means it is easy to lose sight of the importance of their teammates. For a cyclist to win a particular stage, though, they rely on their teammates to support them by cycling in a particular formation, which allows the team's main contender for each stage to conserve energy. They will then have the stamina to finish the stage strongly. Support staff such as team directors, domestiques mechanics, and chefs play a crucial role in achieving success in cycling, perhaps more so than in any other sport.

A popular story in Tour folklore occurred in 1913. Eugene Christophe was leading the overall race by a whopping 18 minutes when he experienced a problem with his bike. He was about 10km away from Ste-Marie-de-Campan when he realised that the handlebar fork had broken. At the time, riders were not allowed to get any outside help. He walked the 10km to Ste-Marie-de-Campan carrying his bike whilst the other riders passed him by. When he reached the town, he went straight to the blacksmiths to repair his fork – which was permitted – but Christophe needed both hands to undertake the repair, which meant he was unable to fan the flames of the fire and keep it hot enough to mould the metal.

In order to complete the repair, Christophe asked a young boy to man the bellows and keep the fire going, and eventually, Christophe was able to return to the race. By this time, he had lost four hours of time, and his dream of winning the Tour had literally gone up in smoke. When Christophe crossed the finish line, race organisers congratulated him on his achievement in fixing the broken fork but advised him that by using the boy to keep the fire going, he had enlisted outside help and would be given a ten-minute penalty. Fans were up in arms, and after several protests, the penalty was reduced to three minutes, but that did little to console Christophe. He still ended up finishing in seventh place overall.

Over the years, the Tour has developed, and it is now the world's largest annual sporting event, attracting 12 million spectators and 3.5 billion television viewers.

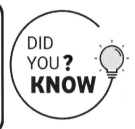

Statistics:

- The race features 176 cyclists who make up 22 teams of 8 riders.
- Substitute riders are not permitted. If any of the cyclists are injured, the team must continue with reduced numbers.
- The overall climb is 48,000 metres, which is equivalent to climbing Mont Blanc ten times.
- The 21 stages comprise nine flat, three hilly and seven mountain stages (including five summits) plus two individual time trials.

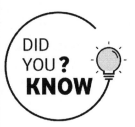
Another strike occurred more recently in 2021 when riders protested on safety grounds following several pile-ups earlier in the Tour.

5. How to Win the Race

The cyclist who completes the 21 stages in the fastest time is the overall winner. In order to determine this, the time for every rider during every stage is recorded and then added together to achieve one cumulative time at the end of the 23 days.

It is, therefore, difficult to tell, when watching any stage, what the gap is between the overall leader and the riders behind them.

The ongoing leader is the rider who wears the coveted 'yellow jersey'. At the end of each stage, the rider's cumulative times are reviewed, and the cyclist currently posting the fastest overall time goes into the next stage as the leader – and wears the jersey. This doesn't necessarily mean they will race out in front, though. Often, the most beneficial way for riders to race is to remain within their team formation and the peloton (main group of cyclists).

In 2022, the overall winner, Danish cyclist Jonas Vingegaard, took 87 hours, 20 minutes and 5 seconds to complete all 21 stages. In second place was the Slovenian rider Tadej

Pogacar, who was three minutes and 34 seconds behind. If you consider the overall time taken, this margin of less than four minutes represents only 0.06% of the entire race – which is barely any time at all.

In 1989, two-time winner Laurent Fignon entered the final stage with a lead of 50 seconds, but he was beaten by his closest rival, Greg LeMond, who ended up crossing the finish line 8 seconds ahead of Fignon. The reason LeMond was able to do this, was down to the aerobars (handlebar extensions) he had added to his bike. These allowed him to ride in a more aerodynamic position, which was further assisted by a sleek new aerodynamic helmet. Aerobars are now only permitted on time-trial bikes during the time-trial stages.

6. Prize Money

The Tour de France has always awarded prize money:

- In its first year, the prize for the winner was 20,000 French francs.
- Between 1976 and 1987, the cash prize for winning was replaced by an apartment that the race sponsor provided.
- In 1988, the first prize was a car, a studio apartment, a work of art and 500,000 French francs!
- The first rider to cross the Col du Galabier, where the monument to Henri Desgrange stands, is awarded a souvenir of Henri Desgrange (in memory of the founder).
- Today, the winner of the Tour de France collects 500,000 Euros, which is equivalent to about £560,000. The second-placed cyclist receives 200,000 Euros, while the third-place finisher wins 100,000 Euros.
- As it is a team sport, it is customary for winners to split their prize money with the other members of their team.
- A rider who wins a stage will receive a prize of 11,000 Euros. The cyclists who win the points classification and mountain classifications (other competitions for which riders compete for points by finishing in the top 15 in given stages and reaching the top of certain mountains first) both receive 25,000 Euros.
- Money can also be earned during the sprint races and specific climbs, and prizes are awarded to the four best young riders.

7. Choosing the Route

The general director of the Tour, Christian Prudhomme, is in charge of everything related to the Tour; however, it is the race director, Thierry Gouvenou, who selects the route. He must also decide where the climbs and sprints will be and manage all the details that make up the race. As the current race director, Gouvenou relishes this task because he has a penchant for maps and geography.

The organisers do not charge spectators to watch the race and are committed to taking the Tour across all regions of France every few years. Every year, the route takes a huge amount of planning, and if a town is interested in hosting part of the Tour de France one year, they can submit a letter to the Amaury Sports Organisation (ASO) requesting to be an arrival or departure point. Tour planners then visit the town to see if it can handle such a large event. If they are subsequently selected to host the start of a stage, they must pay a sizeable fee of no less than £50,000 (often considerably more) for the privilege.

To host the finish of a stage, the rate is doubled to no less than £100,000. Allegedly, London paid well over £2 million in fees just to host the Grand Depart (the start of the whole Tour) in 2007. The French make a big deal of the start; it resembles a circus, which gets underway on the eve of the first day of the race. Hosting any part of the race is very prestigious for the chosen town, and often, the entire location will shut down for the day.

The Tour de France route has always featured several iconic mountain stages such as Alpe d'Huez, Mont Ventoux, Col du Galibier and the Col du Tourmalet. It has also, since 1975, finished on the Champs-Elysées in Paris every year.

8. A Stage Itself

The unofficial start of a stage is a purely ceremonial affair and is mostly an opportunity for the host town to gain exposure. After ceremonially signing on (and being introduced to the crowd), riders will usually assemble in the most attractive part of the town. The race leaders are usually front and centre, flanked by local dignitaries (who have paid for the privilege) and usually the local mayor, who will 'drop the flag' to signal the start of the stage.

Once the stage has officially 'started', the race convoy proceeds at a modest pace towards the 'real' start (depart reel), which is located just outside of the town and clear of messy junctions, level crossings and tram lines. It will also be on a nice straight stretch of road. The riders follow the race director's car to this 'real' start, where, if all is well, the race director, standing up through the sunroof, will drop his flag, allowing the cyclists to roll through and pull away to start the race. At this point, anybody could be in front, but it will usually be those who intend to get into a breakaway group or riders looking to prevent others from getting ahead who lead the way.

The Tour de France often looks like a hectic free-for-all as a tightly packed group of riders fly through the French countryside. Right from the start, the vast majority of the riders will form a large peloton (group), with cyclists jostling to form a breakaway. If successful, that rider will be joined by a few more but it takes a huge amount of effort to break away from the rest. This is because the workload is only shared between a few riders as opposed to those in the peloton who can share the load between maybe 160 cyclists. Often the breakaway pack will contain riders from several different competing teams who will be forced to work together by switching places to share the brunt of the wind pressure that is present at the front of the pack.

Once a breakaway group is established, the next part of the race becomes a game of cat and mouse. Those still cycling in the peloton must decide when and if to rein in the breakaway group. A lot will depend on where the serious contenders (and their teammates) are. It is unlikely that the main contenders for the whole Tour will be in a breakaway, but they might ask one or two teammates to join it to help influence their strategy. Influencing the group is achieved by slowing it down if they are leading it or not taking their turn to lead and forcing others to expend more energy.

When it comes to reining in the breakaway, those in the peloton will draw on their experience, advice from their team director and the nature of the stage itself. Often, they make their move with about 30 kilometres left, and sometimes, they only manage to catch the breakaway with a few hundred metres to go before the end of the stage.

You may think that all stages start where the previous one finished, but the cyclists often, in fact, have to take a long boat, train or car journey to get to the next starting line.

9. The Jerseys

Overall Race Leader – Yellow Jersey

Immediately after World War I, Desgrange introduced the yellow jersey (maillot jaune) to be worn by the overall race leader. It was no coincidence that he chose yellow. He did so for two reasons: first, the roadside spectators (and now camera drones) could easily pick out the race leader, and second, perhaps more significantly (in a stroke of marketing genius), L'Auto happened to be printed on yellow paper. What a coincidence!

Top Sprinter - Green Jersey

The sprinters own the road on flat stages and aim to claim the green jersey. Colloquially known as the sprinter's jersey, this award goes to the rider who has scored the most points so far in the Tour. Points are earned by finishing in the top 15 in given stages.

To tilt the classification in favour of 'pure' sprinters (riders who tend to fall off the back on mountainous days), more points are offered in stages that the organiser deems to be 'flat.'

Best Young Rider - White Jersey

This classification is similar to the yellow jersey, but it is exclusively for riders younger than 26 years old. On rare occasions, like in 2019, a phenomenal young rider (the 22 year old Columbian, Bernal), was eligible to wear both the yellow and white jerseys.

King of the Mountains– Polka Dot Jersey

The King of the Mountains competition awards climbers who escape in the Alps and Pyrenees and beat their rivals to the top of France's biggest climbs. The Tour began designating a 'King of the Mountains' award in 1933 to honour the rider who collects the most points over the course of the race on chosen climbs.

The categorisation system is opaque and subjective; for example, sometimes, a climb's categorisation is influenced by where it falls during a stage's route.

The polka dot jersey (which was introduced in 1975 and is worn by the King of the Mountains rider) may have seemed an odd design choice. As is usually the case with the Tour, the decision was a financial one and was chosen by the chocolate company Chocolat Poulain. Their packaging comprised distinctive polka dot wrappers, which meant that the sponsorship gave them a great deal of publicity.

National Road Race Champions

National road race champions wear the colours of their nation in 'ordinary' stages, and national time trial champions in time trials.

The World Champion

They wear a jersey with horizontal stripes in their team's colours during the race.

The Lanterne Rouge

There is another award (of dubious merit) known as the Lanterne Rouge (red lantern). The title is awarded by Tour photographers looking for good pictures to sell. There is no Jersey, and the award is given to the rider who has taken the most time to complete the Tour. It is red in colour to represent the red light at the back of a vehicle so that it can be seen in the dark. It often garners such sympathy that the rider can command high fees.

10. The Classification of the Climbs

Throughout the Tour, riders climb many mountains in both the Pyrenees and the Alps. The Tour classifies climbs (hills to you and me) according to how difficult they are, as previously mentioned. The lower its category, the harder the climb, which means riders can achieve more points during these stages. Cyclists are also awarded more points on mountaintop stage finishes, especially if they win the stage.

Note: Gradient percentage denotes how much you climb versus the distance travelled. A gradient of 6%, for example, means that for every 100 metres the rider travels in forward, they will climb six metres in height.

Category 4: The easiest climbs. They usually need to be at least 4km long with a gradient of at least 4% (or a steeper gradient and shorter distance).

Category 3: Things are getting a little tougher here. As a rule, there is a 6% gradient for 4km or so, and sometimes, shorter distances have an 8% gradient.

Category 2: Longer climbs that are sometimes steeper. Generally, more than 5km at 7% gradient or longer than 10km at around 5%.

Category 1: Roughly 5-10km at 8% gradient or 15km+ at 6%.

HC or 'Hors Category': This is a slick French term which means the climb is above categorisation. These are long climbs - 15km to 30km – and are steep and brutal. At least 15km of the ride will be above 8% gradient.

Subjectivity of the Climbs

Despite all the numbers, the categorisation of a climb can also be subjective and may be influenced by organisers who simply 'feel' that the climb is harder. Or, if a category 1 climb comes at the end of a stage, for example, it may be re-classified to HC to take into account the rider's physical condition and energy levels.

11. Rules

Competing in the Tour de France involves navigating two sets of rules: the **official regulations** and the **unwritten ones**. Though most competitive sports have 'unwritten rules', it's difficult to find another with as many as the Tour de France. Some of the rules seem outdated yet there are Tour de France purists who still view these as a charming aspect of the event. Many traditions, some of which date back to the early days, have thus survived.

Some of these unofficial rules include:

- Don't attack the yellow jersey (race leader) on the last stage, even if you're only seconds behind in the general classification. This means that the race effectively ends on the penultimate stage.

- If the Tour passes through a town where one of the competitors lives, he will often get off his bike to say 'hi' to friends and family. He will let other riders know he intends to do this, and the peloton will slow down, letting him rejoin at the back without the others taking advantage.

- Riders don't 'attack' the yellow jersey whilst the rider is relieving himself or if he has a puncture. To do so would be considered bad form. After all, they might need help later in the Tour.

- Riders don't attack competitors in a feed zone.

- Riders don't attack the yellow jersey or other leading contenders if they crash or experience a mechanical incident.

- If a rider is catching up (for example, after a puncture), he can draft behind team cars or take a 'sticky bottle' (holding onto a bottle just a little longer than strictly necessary) to get back to the main bunch (the peloton).

- Race leaders and experienced riders in a peloton can call riders to go slow if they perceive race conditions to be dangerous.

There is a rumour that the categories for the mountain stages relate to the gears that were needed for a Citroen 2CV to navigate the hills.

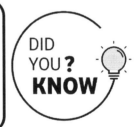

DID YOU **?** **KNOW**

12. Why Do Unofficial Rules Still Exist?

It may seem strange that a sport like cycling, with its long history of cheating (including drug use and doping), also has a strong ethos of honourable racing within the professional peloton. The ethos probably exists because of the extreme demands and dangers of professional cycling.

13. The Rise & Fall of Lance Armstrong

How many TDF riders can you name?

Bradley Wiggins and Chris Froome are two of the most well-known household names,particularly in the UK. Some may have heard of the legendary Eddie Merckx, who holds many of the Tour's records. But everyone (whether into cycling or not) will almost certainly have heard of Lance Armstrong.

Lance Armstrong won a stage in the 1993 and 1995 Tours. A year later, in 1996, he was diagnosed with testicular cancer and given a slim chance of living since it had also spread to various parts of his body and brain. Following an operation and painful chemotherapy, he fought back and incredibly won the whole Tour in 1999. From then, and defying the odds, he never looked back and joined the élite club of Anquetil, Merckx, Hinault and Indurain by winning five Tours - before going two better.

Sadly, (for Armstrong), he was later stripped of all of his TDF wins and titles following the conclusion of a lengthy doping investigation. He was found to have taken performance-enhancing drugs and was banned from cycling events for life in 2012. He has since (after surviving cancer) dedicated his life to charity projects.

As an American, Lance Armstrong's fall from grace overshadowed the sport somewhat, to the point that the French, in particular, are now suspicious of any winner who is not of French descent.

DID YOU ? KNOW

All Tour de France cyclists are drug tested at the start of the tour and a random six athletes are chosen for testing at the finish line and hotels after each stage. Stage winners and race leaders are tested every day.

14. Rider Strategies & Tactics

Drafting

This is probably the most important aspect of how the race is conducted. To best explain, imagine you are riding on your own, battling with a headwind; it is tough. When, though, you are riding in a group, this pain is shared as many riders will take it in turn to lead the group. This is known as drafting. The rider at the front bears all the resistance of a headwind, which reduces the wind resistance and amount of energy needed for those behind. The idea is that over the course of a ride, everyone in the group experiences the benefits of drafting by rotating the lead rider. If this is done well, it can reduce the effort needed by up to a massive 30% - which explains why cyclists like to ride in a Peloton. To get the maximum benefit riders need to be within a few centimetres of the one in front, although some benefit will be gained by being a bike length behind.

Wind direction also plays a crucial role in riders' positioning. Riders naturally switch formations to ensure that as few riders as possible bear the brunt of the wind. When it is time for the lead rider to end their shift, they signal that they are going to move to the back of the peloton by pointing in the direction they intend to travel.

'Echelon' refers to a riding formation utilised by a group of cyclists to combat side winds. The riders stagger themselves, creating a diagonal line across the road, which allows them to shelter each other from the wind and maintain their pace while conserving energy.

Breakaways

Riders are very strategic and don't cycle as fast as they can throughout the whole race. They tend to cycle in the main peloton, but occasionally, smaller groups will break away from it. This technique, known as a breakaway, can be advantageous for cyclists who may not be particularly skilled at climbing hills or sprinting, as it provides them with an opportunity to win a stage. A breakaway consisting of six riders can, in some ways, be more efficient, particularly when going through a town, as they can negotiate a roundabout (for example) more easily than a peloton of 160 riders.

Attacks

Attacks occur during climbs when a rider suddenly breaks away from the peloton at high speed, hoping to leave others behind.

15. Key Decisions & Information for the Riders & Teams

- Whether to leave the peloton to form a breakaway group and, if so, when.

- Whether to chase a rider who has escaped the peloton.

- For each stage of the Tour, the teams will estimate the likely number of calories that riders will burn. For example, in one stage, which included two climbs of the famous Mont Ventoux, the German rider Andre Greipel burned 6,080 calories.

- The teams have to consider how and when to give their riders the calories they will need throughout the tour.

- The teams will review the entire stage to determine when and where their riders will need nutrition, depending on whether they are sitting in a peloton or riding up a steep climb.

- The fundamental decision facing the riders is to make sure that they run out of energy as they near the top of the mountain so that they can recharge a little on the way back down.

16. Teams & their Strategies

The Tour is a test of endurance, strength and skill, but it can also be won or lost with the right strategies or tactics. The world's best teams pick the stages that suit their riders and try to strike at the perfect moment.

One of the most successful teams of recent years is the Sky team, led by Dave Brailsford. He was certainly a detail man and went to such lengths as having bikes altered specifically for when the Tour went over cobbles and hiring a Spanish coach to improve communication with his Spanish riders. He also looked for marginal gains outside of the races, such as vacuuming riders' hotel rooms to cut down on infection, transporting individual mattresses, and using dehumidifiers, air conditioning units, and filters in their rooms.

Teams settle on their tactics prior to the race by assessing their strengths and weaknesses and working out ways to succeed. Here are some examples of how teams might set their strategies and how they might execute them:

i.   Team with a top **General Classification** rider: This team hopes to win the overall race. To do this, they will need to deal with flat and rolling stages to allow energy conservation for key mountain stages and individual time trials. The leader's teammates will join them in breakaways so that their rider won't spend energy chasing others all day. They'll also set up the team leader to attack on key climbs or at least follow his rivals to defend his position.

ii.   Team with a top **Sprinter**: To win the green jersey (awarded to the top sprinter), a team will target the flat stages. These can be any stage within the overall race, and to prevent specialist sprinters from ignoring the mountain stages, the organisers set a maximum time allowed for all riders to complete every stage, including those riders aiming for the green jersey. This is based on a proportion of the time taken by the winner of each stage. Naturally, no one knows how long this will be at the outset of a stage, and those aiming for the green jersey must complete all stages within this maximum time. If they don't, they are eliminated from the whole Tour, thereby foregoing the chance to win any stage. On mountain stages, a team with a top sprinter might have to call riders back from the peloton to help pace their sprinter to the finish so he doesn't get time cut from the overall race.

iii. Team with **Top Climbers**: The King of the Mountains (KOM) classification is given to the rider who is awarded the most points for reaching the top of certain mountains first. The leader is known as the King of the Mountains and, since 1975, has worn the polka dot jersey. This classification is less of an obvious team effort; however, it is advantageous to have a teammate in the breakaway on a key mountain stage when points are up for grabs. Also, when helping a teammate who is trying to win the jersey, teammates can contest the climbs and finish ahead of KOM rivals to spoil their attempt to take over the lead.

iv.   Smaller teams **without a top contender**: These teams usually try to put a rider in the day's breakaway. This could earn them the Combativity Prize (awarded for the most aggressive rider) or, if they play their cards right, a stint in a leader's jersey or even a stage win. Their sponsors will benefit from the publicity of a rider being at or near the front because television cameras usually focus on the leaders. This strategy requires constant attacking in the early kilometres of the race, something that most fans rarely see on a broadcast. It is a hectic, painful part of the stage, but it's crucial in establishing a breakaway. Meanwhile, a breakaway rider's teammates might patrol the front of the peloton to disrupt the chase.

An Individual Sport with Teams or a Team Sport with Individuals?

Why are there teams if only one rider can win the Tour de France?

As alluded to earlier, professional road cycling has a curious tension between the team and the individual. The key thing to remember is this: if a cyclist wins one of the prestigious classification titles or even holds a leader's jersey for a single stage, it is viewed as a team success.

Though only one cyclist will stand on the podium, it is usually with the assistance of their teammates, and therefore, a win for one rider is a win for the team.

Teammates offer assistance to their main rider by:

- Getting into breakaways so their leader doesn't have to work to chase the breakaway.
- Chasing down breakaways to give the leader a chance to win.
- Retrieving food and water for the leader or other key riders.
- Pacing the leader up key climbs – although drafting isn't as crucial on hills, it can still be a psychological advantage to have a teammate at your side.
- If the leader were to suffer a crash or breakdown, he might need help to get back to the main peloton. Without teammates to draft, it might be nearly impossible to rejoin the peloton.
- Giving the leader their bike or a wheel in the event of a mechanical problem. This can often be quicker than waiting for a team car or neutral support to show up with a spare.

Support

While watching bike racing, we tend to focus on the riders, the crashes, the punctures, the chases, the attacks and the victories. However, it's important to remember that every rider has a support team behind them. These are made up of dozens of moving parts, any of which could be the difference between success and failure. These unsung members of the riders' support team put in a lot of effort during races and training camps to ensure that the riders achieve the best possible results. The support riders are known as domestiques, which, as mentioned earlier, is the French term for helper.

The priority is not where the domestique is in the race but the assistance that they can provide to their team. They aim to keep their top riders safe, fed and watered. They will often chase down breakaways or attempt to dictate the general pace of a peloton. The domestiques sacrifice any opportunity to win the entire race, including individual stages, in pursuit of the overall team objectives.

Several domestiques have become famous in their own right. For instance, Lucien Aimar supported Jacques Anquetil, then went on to win the Tour himself in 1966. In 1986, Greg LeMond won the 1986 Tour de France after being Bernard Hinault's domestique the previous year, and Chris Froome achieved the same feat in 2013 after supporting Bradley Wiggins in his 2012 Olympic year.

The riders are also supported by teams of mechanics whose role is to make sure every rider's bike is properly tuned. They will pack the roofs of their support vehicles so that if an important rider suffers a mechanical problem, his replacement bike will be accessible. The mechanics can often salvage a bad day. The French rider Romain Bardet recently suffered three punctured tyres on cobblestones and yet was able to minimise the time lost because his mechanics were quick to give him a new wheel when he needed it.

Teamwork is perhaps most critical in the mountains. When a team takes to the Alps, expect to see teammates near their team leader at all times, doing as much work as they can for their man for as long as their legs will hold out. Having a teammate or two on difficult climbs is often what makes a great rider a champion. Whenever a rival would try to attack by accelerating away from Froome up a steep slope, Thomas would chase the rival and take Froome with him. This made the ride for Froome easier as he was able to conserve energy behind Thomas while keeping the attacker in sight.

A great team can also advance to the front of the peloton and keep the pace relentlessly high, eliminating an attack before it begins.

Depending on the type of stage, anyone (including a yellow jersey contender) could act as a domestique. For example, on a flat stage, when there isn't much time to gain, a pure climber might do domestique duties so that sprinters who are capable of winning the stage can focus on riding their fastest. When the terrain gets bumpier, the roles often reverse.

<u>Support cars</u>

Each team is allowed to have two support vehicles following the peloton. The order of the cars is determined by the order of a team's leading rider. These cars are allowed to provide refreshments, change bikes, assist with breakdowns and provide medical help. There are also cars for the organisers and special guests. These cars do not pose a risk to the riders as they are generally well behind the peloton. However, if there is a breakaway group which is more than 30 seconds ahead of the main peloton, cars are allowed in the gap. If that gap were to shrink, the cars would be ordered back.

17. Communication

Race radio: During the Tour, race organisers use a one-way communication system called race radio. Often, team cars cannot get close to their riders, so they use race radio to inform them of any crashes or if any riders have pulled away from the peloton. This information allows team cars to speed ahead and assist their riders.

Car-to-car radio: There is a channel which is only open to the two team cars on the course so that they can speak to each other. Amidst so much chaos, the two must be in constant contact to determine who to help and whether to pull over and swap rider-specific equipment. The cars that follow the peloton do so according to the team rankings, meaning that the top-ranked team is first in line to help their riders with mechanical failures or even punctures.

Car-to-rider radio: There is also a channel that allows race directors to talk directly to their riders. The Tour imposes strict limits on the data that can be transmitted to riders during a race, and in fact, the governing body (the UCI) tried to ban two-way radio communication but backed off in the face of opposition from teams and their riders.

This facility has been available since the mid-90s, although some in the sport want to abolish it, claiming that it has eliminated spontaneity in favour of robotic coordination and tactics. The riders generally like it, though, and teams insist that the radio is used almost entirely for communicating times and potential hazards ahead and that little collusion takes place.

18. Neutral Service Cars

The Tour is such a massive event and, therefore, needs a matching support set-up. The Tour organisers provide roughly 200 cars, which are manned by neutral drivers and technicians – i.e. they don't have an affiliation with any team. These cars move around the peloton sorting out mechanical issues that would otherwise take riders out of the competition and are also on hand in case of an accident. Each team is only allowed two support vehicles of their own, so more often than not, the rider's own mechanics are too far away from incidents, which is why these 'neutral' cars play such an important role. The Tour features many varied challenges for the riders and their bikes, including cobblestones, mountains, tight bends and steep declines, all of which can put different strains on the bikes, thus increasing the risk of mechanical issues and accidents.

19. How To Win If You Don't Win

Here is another way that the Tour de France can trip up novices. Unlike a typical sport where 'winning' is the goal for all riders, there are multiple secondary prizes available during the course of the race's three weeks. Some teams and riders don't even bother vying for the yellow jersey and instead focus their energy on these other prizes. These other 'prizes' are denoted by helmets or numbers, which are worn in the same way as the jersey so that other riders and cameras can see them clearly. What the helmets mean:

Best Team Classification - Yellow Helmets

Although this classification has existed since 1930, it is often overlooked by casual fans and rarely influences how riders or teams race. Like the yellow or white jerseys, this award is given based on overall time in the race. Each team tabulates the finish times of its three best riders on every stage, with the team leading this classification having its riders wearing yellow helmets.

Most Aggressive Rider - Red Number

Also known as the Combativity Award, mentioned briefly earlier, this is often the most mysterious prize in the Tour. In every stage (except time trials), a jury decides which rider is the most aggressive (usually the one who has been attacking a lot and gambling on a breakaway). Later in the broadcast, the announcers award the Combativity prize, so if you spot a rider with a red number on their jersey, then he was named the most aggressive rider for the previous stage. At the end of the Tour, one rider gets the Super Combativity award.

20. How Does a Time Trial (TT) Work?

Most of the stages in the Tour involve all cyclists starting at the same time and riding to a finish line, making it easy to see who is at the front and how far behind the others are. The time trials are different, however, because the riders set off at one-minute intervals. Typically, the starting order of riders is determined by their position in the overall GC rankings, with the rider in last place starting first and the rider with the yellow jersey going out last. Time trials (which are usually between 5 and 30km distance) often prove decisive in determining the overall winner of the Tour. In 2020, the twentieth (and penultimate) stage of the Tour was a mountain time trial, and Tadej Pogacar overturned a 57-second deficit to win the overall Tour.

Time trials are not always welcomed among fans, though. Many spectators and pundits consider the solo discipline boring, especially when compared with the tactical thrills of mountain racing and sprints. Time trials can be more challenging for the riders, too, because they will be riding against themselves with no knowledge of how their competitors are performing. This makes it more of a mental discipline and an ultimate test of a cyclist's ability.

The first stage in modern Tours is often a short time trial to decide who will wear the yellow jersey on the following day. There are usually two or three time-trials during the Tour, with the last one often being the penultimate stage. Also, in time trials, there is a wider variation in stage completion times between the riders due to their respective abilities. It's worth noting here too, that if a rider catches up with the competitor ahead, he is not permitted to 'draft' and must overtake as soon as possible.

21. The Final Stage

Every year since 1975, the final stage of the Tour de France has concluded on the iconic Champs-Élysées in Paris. As the peloton arrives in central Paris, the French Air Force provides a three-jet flypast with the colours of the French tricolour in smoke behind them.

The stage typically starts on the outskirts of Paris, and teams agree on a truce for the opening portion of the race. Cyclists take the opportunity to have a moment of tranquillity, laugh, and celebrate the achievement of finishing the Tour. It has become customary not to challenge the rider in the yellow jersey on the final stage, although usually, by this stage, he has an unassailable lead. The leader will often pose for photographs and even enjoy a glass of champagne on the way.

As the cyclists approach Paris, the competition intensifies when the sprinters and their teams begin the real race of the day. After all, the last stage is still a race and riders will want to be able to claim a stage win. Upon reaching central Paris, the cyclists enter the Champs-Élysées by riding up the Rue de Rivoli, onto the Place de la Concorde, then turning right onto the Champs-Élysées itself. They then complete eight laps, including cycling around the Arc de Triomphe, down the Champs-Élysées, around the Louvre and across the Place de la Concorde before returning to the Champs-Élysées.

While a number of riders will try to pull away from the peloton on the Champs-Elysées, the chances of success are slim, and these attempts are often seen as one last opportunity for teams to showcase their colours. It is extremely hard for a small group to resist the push of chasing sprinter's teams on the stage's flat circuit, and the overwhelming majority of Tours have ended up in a mass sprint.

Occasionally, when a rider has reached a significant milestone during the Tour, it is customary for the peloton to let him enter the Champs-Elysées section of the stage in first place. American George Hincapie was bestowed such an honour in 2012 in recognition of his final and record-setting 17th Tour de France.

22. The Caravan

When national teams were introduced in 1930, race organisers were responsible for accommodating riders, so to fund the cost, Henri Desgrange allowed advertisers to precede the race. Seeing the Tour de France live is a thrill for any true fan. The French countryside is full of TDF fans lining the route, sometimes waiting hours for just a few seconds glimpse of the speeding peloton. With upwards of a million spectators lining the routes, the TDF organisers devised one of the most colourful and noisy marketing mediums, the Tour Caravan, to maximise advertising exposure. These caravans are covered in garish adverts and are certainly an eye-catching sight.

A few years ago, a friend persuaded me to join him and six others for a 'holiday' cycling in the Alps to coincide with the Tour. The idea was to ride for five days and then pitch up to watch the caravan first, followed by the riders themselves. Knowing how fast the riders would pass, we attempted to pick a spot where they had to slow down for a steep bend and a long climb ahead. We sat and waited and waited. About four hours later, we heard the noise of the Caravan, and I stood in awe as my first 'caravan' trundled past – in a hail storm of cheap trinkets – watching on as fans young and old risked life and limb to pick up said junk from the smouldering pavement before getting squashed by a giant weird looking vehicle.

23. Some Famous Quotes

Jacques Anquetil - after winning a race by twelve seconds

"It was eleven more than necessary."

Lance Armstrong

"Pain is temporary. Quitting lasts forever."

24. Interesting Facts

★ Most who get into a breakaway don't expect to win the stage, but they benefit from the publicity, with the cameras following the breakaway group for many hours. Often, breakaway riders are trying to make a name for themselves and for their sponsors.

★ The teams will have two cars on the route, carrying all manner of spares and nutrition. When beside a rider, they can offer advice.

★ Some time trials include hills, whilst others are flat.

★ Time trials are totally different to ordinary stages as it is not possible to take advantage of being in a peloton. Also, you are on your own, and it is just the rider against the clock. He has no idea how the others are performing.

★ Independent service companies line the route, particularly on the narrow parts, to offer their services to riders. They can and do help when the teams' cars cannot get to their riders by lending wheels, etc. Riders have to hope, though, that any spares offered by these companies are compatible with their bikes!

★ There are 'feed zones' providing bananas, water, electrolytes and jelly babies.

25. In Summary - The Essence of the Tour de France

The Tour de France is essentially the World Cup of road cycling.

It attracts millions of fans who line the streets to watch their heroes for a few seconds as well as many more millions who watch the stages unfold on television. In fact, the Tour de France is the third most-watched sporting event behind the Olympics and the Football World Cup. The riders race in all weathers and over all terrains, making it gruelling both physically and mentally.

With only two rest days throughout the entire event, the Tour de France really is the pinnacle of cycling fitness and of any rider's career.

A Few Notable Records:

★ Most Tour Wins
   • Lance Armstrong ~ 7 (he was stripped of them all following his doping scandal)
   • Miguel Inurain ~ 5
   • Eddy Merckx ~ 5
   • Bernard Hinault ~ 5
   • Jacques Anquetil ~ 5
   • Chris Froome ~ 4

★ Most stage wins

- Mark Cavendish ~ 34
- Eddy Merckx ~ 34
- Bernard Hinault ~ 28
- Andre Leducq ~ 25
- Andre Darrigade ~ 22

Chapter Seven

TENNIS

"Tennis is mostly mental; you win or lose the match before you go out on court."

Venus Williams

CONTENTS

1. What is Tennis?

Tennis is a racquet sport played between two people (singles) or two pairs (doubles). Players use a racquet strung with cord and hit a hollow rubber ball covered with yellow felt. In this chapter, I am going to concentrate on singles. Many rules, customs and strategies are the same for both versions; however, in doubles, the playing area is larger, and the reaction times needed are even shorter. The reason for this decision is to give you the gist of how the game is played and the quirks of the sport, as well as to explain some of the key decisions. Hopefully, you will get some idea, and adding doubles only complicates matters – which is definitely not the premise of this book!

The aim of the game is to win points by hitting a tennis ball over a net and into the opponent's court, forcing your opponent to make an error or be unable to return the ball over the net and into your court.

DID YOU **?** **KNOW**

Tennis was once ruled by the MCC (Marylebone Cricket Club), though this is no longer the case. In 1972, a group of professional players launched a new governing body, the Association of Tennis Professionals (ATP).

'Tennis' comes from the French formal imperative form of the verb 'tenir', which means 'to hold'. When a player is about to serve, they 'hold' the ball aloft in preparation, which indicates to their opponent that they are about to serve them the ball.

2. Equipment

*   A tennis racquet.
*   Tennis balls.
*   A tennis court.
*   A net.

The length of a racquet is measured from the bottom of the handle to the tip of the head. It ranges between 27 inches (68.5 cm) and 29 inches (73.5 cm), which is the maximum length allowed.

In France in the 1870s, Pierre Babolat (still a famous name associated with making tennis racquets) had an established business making strings for musical instruments. In 1875, he turned his attention to the up-and-coming sport of lawn tennis and began making racquet strings from sheep intestines. These were the first 'natural gut' tennis strings, and equivalents are still used today. The natural gut is elastic, flexible and keeps the tension in the racquet which is needed to play the game. This tension helps the player to maintain control and power over their shots. In the 1950s, synthetic strings started appearing, but now most racquet strings are made of polyester.

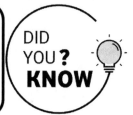

The term 'racquet' is derived from the Arabic word 'rakhat' meaning 'palm of the hand'.

Over time, the strings soften, and as every point in tennis is vitally important, professional players often want to replace their strings. To do this, they will change their racquet (and, by definition, their strings) usually when the tennis balls are changed. This is because the new balls travel faster, and players want their racquet strings to be able to cope.

Racquet Grips

There are multiple ways to hold (grip) a tennis racquet and players will use different grips for different shots in order to affect its outcome. As the game is fast-paced, players continually have to change grips in between shots.

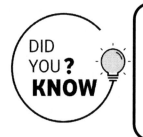

A player will often take six to eight racquets onto the court, each having the strings set to a different tension.

3. How Tennis Began

A long time ago, there was a sport known as 'Real Tennis' which was and still is, played indoors. It began in Tudor times and bears some resemblance to the modern game. In 1874, Lawn tennis began outdoors and adopted many of the rules from Real Tennis.

In 1877, the first major competition took place at Wimbledon in London, and much of the modern terminology used in tennis derives from this period.

4. Where Tennis is Played

The short answer is on a tennis court, which is constructed from one of three main surfaces: **clay**, **grass** or **hard**. The choice of surface affects the speed that the ball travels, the movement needed by the players and the style of play that they adopt.

Hard courts - are made of uniform rigid materials with an acrylic surface layer, the colour of which varies according to the whim of the organisers. They are generally 'faster' (the ball travels faster due to the surface 'bounce') than Clay courts but not quite as fast as Grass courts. The ball bounce is usually fairly predictable and is generally high.

Grass courts – these are the least popular type of court as they are more difficult and expensive to maintain and can only be used in dry weather conditions. They can also be slippery which makes the ball bounce faster and lower and sometimes unpredictably. Grass courts are sown with perennial ryegrass to improve their durability and strength, and the grass at Wimbledon (probably the most famous of all grass courts) is cut to a height of just eight millimetres, which is considered the optimal height for play.

Clay courts – these are iconic and by far the most widely used, mainly due to the low cost of building them. The courts are not actually made of clay but are red in colour because the top layer is made from crushed bricks, and the presence of iron oxide within gives them the rusted clay look. Clay courts are particularly common in Europe and South America with the balls typically bouncing slower and higher. This favours strong baseline players who like to play with a lot of topspin. Another key feature is that clay courts allow players to slide, meaning they can 'get back' shots more easily than on other surfaces.

If a player doubts a call from an official, they can challenge it (more later), but on a clay court, instead of using Hawk-Eye, the Umpire steps down from the chair and looks at where the ball landed. At the end of each set, the court is 'raked' to remove any bounce and slide marks.

All tennis courts have the same dimensions, which are:

Length - 78 ft or 23.77 m
Width - 27ft or 8.23m (singles),
36ft or 10.97m (doubles)

The service box is 21ft long x 13.5 ft wide (6.4 m x 4.11 m)

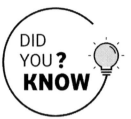

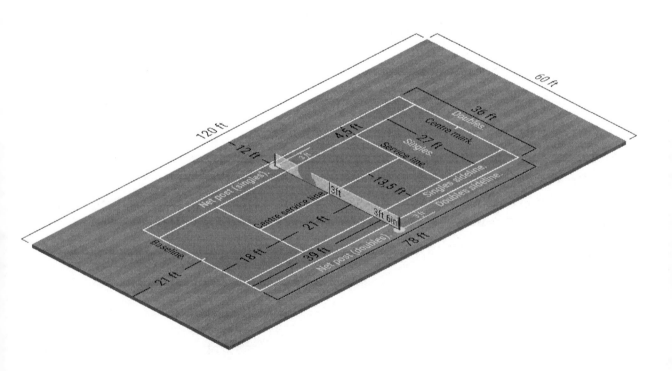

DIMENSIONS OF A TENNIS COURT

5. The Point of Tennis

To win a tennis match, a player needs to accumulate sufficient points to win a game. Then they need to win enough games to win a set and then enough sets to win the match – this will be explained in more detail later. A tennis match is over when the umpire declares, "Game, set, and match to Player X."

Tennis is gladiatorial (intense and hard-fought). In the singles game, there is a Women's event and a Men's event, meaning that on the court, men play men and women play women. The participants cannot have any outside help whilst on court. They will have plenty of help before the match, devising a strategy with the help of their coach, but once the match has started, they are on their own. In some sports, a manager or coach can help a player during a match (such as at half-time), but not in tennis. If plan A is not working, they and they alone need to devise a plan B.

Recently, there have been experiments allowing coaches to offer brief instructions and use gestures to help, but they still cannot have a conversation with their player. The important point - and the main reason why - is to prevent the game from slowing down. In the US Open in 2022, the US Tennis Association allowed coaches to make comments as suggested earlier, but they were not allowed to hold a conversation with players.

As Pete Sampras (one of the all-time greats) famously remarked, *"It's one-on-one out there. There ain't no hiding place. I cannot pass the ball to someone else."*

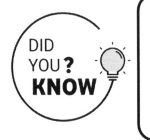

DID YOU? KNOW

According to the International Tennis Federation, a tennis ball must weigh between 56 and 59.4 grams.

6. The Scoring System

Tennis has an unusual scoring system, to say the least. Unlike in football, the score does not go up in units of one or even in units of the same amount. The first point of a game is called 15, the next 30 and the next 40 (not 45). The player who has not scored a point is not 'nil' or 'zero' but 'love'. It is believed that the word 'love' comes from the French term 'oeuf', which means egg and has a similar shape. It's crucial to understand that in order to win a game, a player must be at least two points ahead of their opponent.

If the ball touches a player's body or clothing before landing, their opponent wins the point, even if the ball would have gone out.

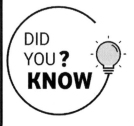

DID YOU **?** **KNOW**

There is a story (which may or may not be true) that the origins of the scoring system come from medieval times in France. There was a game known as 'game of palms' (or in French, 'jeu de paume') in which players used their palms and not a racquet. In this game, players used a court that was 45ft long (as opposed to the modern 39ft). Competitors would start their match at the back of the court until they won a rally, at which time they would be able to move forward (closer to the net and their opponent) by 15ft. If they won a subsequent point, they would only move forward 10ft to avoid ending up on top of the net. This is where the scoring system of 15, 30 and 40 is rumoured to have begun.

There is also a theory that clocks were used to score the early games with the hands being moved to 15, 30 and 45 to denote a winning point. The game would then end when one player's clock reached 60. The 45 score was later changed to 40 to add in an extra point at 50 so that one player could beat their opponent by 2 full points, as per the rules of the game. The score of 50 has become the 'advantage' score from deuce. Whilst this is a popular theory, there is a question over how early the game began as corresponds to the use of clock faces with the quarter hours marked. Essentially, we don't know for certain, how the unusual scoring system came to be.

Winning a game is the first step towards winning a match. A player then needs to win a set. To do this, they must first win six games and, crucially, also be two games ahead of their opponent. Winning a set in tennis is not the same as winning the match. In the main tournaments, matches are played over the best of five sets (for men) and three sets (for women). So, in order to win a match, men need to win three sets. If a player wins a match by three sets to none, they are said to have won in 'straight sets'. If the players are evenly matched, it's not uncommon for men's games to reach the entire five sets and for women's to reach the full three sets.

During a game, when the Umpire calls out the score, they will always call the server's score first. So, if Player A is serving and has won one point and their opponent (the receiver) has won two points, the Umpire will call 15-30. If player A wins the next point, the score will become 30-all. If both players have three points each, the score is called 'deuce', not '40-all'. For this, we are again grateful to the French. I have tried (in vain) to establish why, if the game began in the UK, the French language has so much influence over the terminology and scoring system and come up blank. What I did discover, though, was that the word 'deuce' comes from 'a deux du jeu', which means two points away from winning the game. Whichever player wins the next point, the Umpire will declare they have an advantage. For example, if player A wins that point, the Umpire will call Advantage A. If the player with the advantage then loses the next point, the score returns to deuce. In order to win from deuce, one player must win two points consecutively – an advantage point and the winning point.

Some of you may have noticed that the match score is shown on the television throughout the game. The more observant might have seen the symbol (which looks a bit like a tennis ball) shown beside the name of one of the players. This is an extremely helpful symbol because it appears next to the player who is serving, meaning that even during Wimbledon, when everyone is wearing white, it's relatively easy to figure out who is who!

7. The Match

Before each match begins, the Umpire arranges for a coin to be tossed before they move to a specially designed Umpire's chair which is roughly two metres high and in line with the net. The chair is situated on one side of the court. Whichever player wins the toss can then choose whether they wish to begin the match by serving or receiving.

The other player (who didn't win the toss) gets to choose which end of the court they would like to begin playing from. Both players then have five minutes to warm up together and be ready for play.

Once these five minutes are over, the player serving has one further minute to get settled before being required to serve (hit) the ball to their opponent. To start the match, the Umpire will announce Player A to serve.

How long is a match?

There is no scheduled time for a tennis match. It ends when a player has won a sufficient number of sets. Matches are either the best of three (first to win two) or best of five (first to win three).

Grand Slams are the big tournaments and it is at these that men's matches are played over five sets. In other tournaments throughout the season, the matches are usually played over a maximum of three sets for both men and women. This makes Grand Slams the most challenging tournaments to win.

8. A Game

Each game point begins with a serve. The server needs to hit the ball into the diagonally opposite service box (see earlier diagram) without the ball being stopped by the net. For the first point played, the server always stands on the right-hand side (known as the deuce side) of the court. For the second point, the server moves to the left-hand side of the court (known as the advantage side). The same player continues to serve until the game ends, and then the player who was the receiver becomes the server. This alternates until the conclusion of the match.

'Lets' were once eliminated. Back in 2012, an experiment was carried out at lower-level tournaments to eliminate 'lets' for the first three months of the 2013 season. The experiment didn't last.

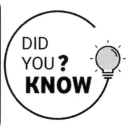
DID YOU ? KNOW

If a server hits the ball at the net but it still lands in the service box, the Umpire will call a 'let'. This means that the Umpire allows the server to take that serve again. There is no limit to the number of lets that can occur. The term' let' has its roots in Old Saxon, where it meant 'to hinder'.

Lets are only used for the service point. Once the ball is in play, any balls that touch the net and land inside the tennis court, are still in play. The rally (back and forth) between opponents then continues in the normal way.

Following the serve, once the ball has landed in the correct service box and the receiver has returned it towards the server, a rally begins. Each player is trying to 'win a point', which is achieved in one of two ways:

- A player forces an error from their opponent, such as hitting the ball into the net or failing to land the ball within the court's boundaries if it goes over the net.
- A player hits the ball into the court, but their opponent is unable to reach it to play a shot. This is known as 'hitting a winner'.

When the two players are engaged in a rally, they are often in a game of cat and mouse, both trying to gain the upper hand. They have to decide in an instant which shot to play. Should they play to their own strengths or the weaknesses of their opponent? Often, it will depend on whether or not they are 'ahead' in a rally.

Once the first game is completed, both players return to their seats (either side of the Umpires' chair). The Umpire will call time after 60 seconds, giving players a further 30 seconds to resume play (the 'break' thus being 90 seconds in total). This process is repeated every two games at which time the players will also change ends. If the number of games played in a set is, therefore, odd, then the players know they are going to be changing ends. They will also change ends after the first game of a new set, even if they changed ends when the previous set had finished. The reason why they change ends is of particular relevance if the match is played outdoors so that both players have to deal with the sun and wind equally.

At the end of each set, there is a longer break of two minutes. Again, the Umpire will call time 30 seconds before play is due to resume.

Toilet Breaks and Medical Timeouts

- Players are allowed one toilet break (of three minutes) or a change of attire break (five minutes) per match. The three minute time begins when a player enters the toilet cubicle and ends when they leave. If a player is changing their attire, they must change all of their clothes - including underwear!

- Players may request a medical timeout at any point in the match for a new acute injury. In theory, a medic is given limitless time to diagnose if the issue is treatable, but the Umpire will want to keep the match on schedule. Once it has been established whether or not the injury is treatable, the player can take a further three minutes (or five if there is blood involved), before they resume play.

As mentioned earlier, each game begins with one of the players serving the ball. The serving player attempts to hit the ball into their opponent's service box by tossing it into the air and hitting it when it is on its way down. If they are successful, a rally begins; if they are not, they get a second chance to do so, known as a second serve.

If that also fails, the point is lost without the opponent needing to play a shot. This is known as a double fault (simply two errors). As mentioned earlier, if the ball hits the net on its way to the service box (on either the first or second serve), the Umpire will call a 'let', and the server has a chance to serve again – and try not to hit the net.

When the server successfully lands the ball into their opponent's service box, it is then up to the receiving player to return the ball and maintain the rally. If the receiver fails to touch the ball with their racquet at all after the serve, the server wins the point, which is known as 'serving an ace'.

Let's pretend we are going to serve the ball. How do you think you would approach it? Would you serve as fast as possible, hoping to win the point with a single shot and overpower your opponent, or would you take some pace off the ball to make sure it lands in the service box?

Imagine it is your turn to serve. You have collected the now customary three or four balls from the ball boy/girl and approached the service position. Before serving, you will discard the unwanted balls, leaving you with one. Now, you bounce your chosen ball, but before you toss it in the air to hit and serve, you have to be absolutely clear in your mind where you are aiming. Do you serve out wide, into your opponent's body or down the middle of the court, close to the centre line?

If you direct your serve to the outside of the court, you will force your opponent to move out wide, which can open up the remainder of the court for your second shot. Although this sounds like a perfect tactic, there is a risk to it. It can give your opponent an angle to hit a winning return.

You could choose to aim at their body, which won't 'open up' the court for your second shot but will ensure that their return is reachable.

The third option is to serve down the middle of the court near the centre line (known as going down the T, due to the T shape towards the back of the court), hoping that your opponent will be unable to reach and return the serve.

Good serving is all about keeping your opponent guessing.

What's interesting, though, is that there isn't a clock for the second serve. I think the reason for this is that the point started with the first serve, so it would be difficult to determine when to start the clock for a second serve.

Also, the clock isn't used after a let, presumably for the same reason.

DID YOU ? KNOW

There is also a time limit between points. Once the Umpire has called the score, the server has 25 seconds to hit their next serve. This rule has been introduced to speed up play. If a player transgresses, they can be warned and if it happens again, a point will be awarded to their opponent. There is a clock next to the scoreboard which counts down from 25 - 0 so that players, officials and spectators can clearly see when a player is close to the time limit. Following a long rally, the Umpire might decide to give the players a bit more recovery time and will delay announcing the score in order to do so.

9. How Does a Tie-Break Work?

Tie breaks are an incredibly important part of tennis matches, and it's surprising how many members of tennis clubs are unsure of how they work.

They were introduced to prevent matches from going on forever, which is good for both players and spectators. No one wants to watch a match for 10 hours! They also add a great deal of drama because every single point is crucial – more so perhaps than in the match itself. When a player wins a point 'against the serve', they are said to have got a 'mini-break'.

When do tie-breaks take place?

When tennis players win six games each, and the set is therefore tied, a tie-break game is played. The process is as follows:

1. The player who would have served the 13th game serves the first point of the tie-break from the deuce court (right-hand side).

2. After the point ends, the other player serves the next two points, serving first from the advantage court (left-hand side) and then secondly from the deuce court (right-hand side).

3. After the third point, the first player serves again, and they continue to swap after every two points until one player has reached seven points AND is two points ahead of their opponent.

4. Serving always starts from the advantage court (apart from the very first point).

5. After six points (and each subsequent six points), the players change ends.

6. Once the tie-break is over, the Umpire will call the set over by declaring the set to Player X by 7 games to 6.

7. To add to the drama, it is possible for one player to have a set point and then, two points later, for the other player to have a match point!

Tie-break variations

Historically, there were no tie-breaks in the final (fifth) set of a Grand Slam. However, the semi-final at Wimbledon in 2018 between John Isner and Kevin Anderson lasted over six and a half hours, with the final set eventually being won by Kevin Anderson 26-24.

This meant that the winner was at a distinct disadvantage for his next match, the final. It was also a bit boring for the spectators. So, the authorities decided to act. All Grand Slams now enforce a tie-break once the score reaches six games all in the final set of any match. The tie-break in a final set differs slightly in that the players need to get ten points to win the set and not seven as in other sets. This decision was not universally popular due to many of the classic matches having featured extended final sets.

10. Challenging a Call

During play, if any part of the ball lands on any part of the line, it is deemed to be 'in' (in play – the ball remains in play, and the rally is to continue). There are up to nine line judges positioned around a court who will determine whether a serve or a shot is in or out. If a player doesn't agree with the decision of an official, they may challenge it, which they do by indicating to the umpire (usually by waving their racquet vaguely towards the Umpire).

If a player indicates that they wish to challenge a call, the Umpire will alert the crowd by saying Player A is challenging a call and whether that call was declared in or out.

Hawk-Eye technology is then used to display a replay of the shot (on a large screen) and a close-up of the line to indicate whether the ball in question was in or out. Hawk-Eye is used at all Grand Slam tournaments, with the exception of Roland Garros, which is played on clay. This is because it is easy to see where the ball has landed on clay courts, although this does increase pressure on the umpires because they need to be fully alert and watch the ball at all times. There is no technology to fall back on.

At the beginning of each set, players are given three challenges. If a player makes an unsuccessful challenge, then they will 'lose' that challenge and thus have only two remaining. Once they have 'lost' their three challenges then they will not be permitted to make any further challenges until the next set. If a player 'wins' the challenge, then they retain their challenge, and this usually means that their opponent will be deducted a point (on the basis that players only challenge on points they have lost).

There are rumours that line judges will be replaced by technology from the 2025 season. This happened quite a bit during COVID-19, and more and more tournaments are dispensing with line judges. John McEnroe is probably suggesting this is about 40 years too late!

11. The Scoreboard

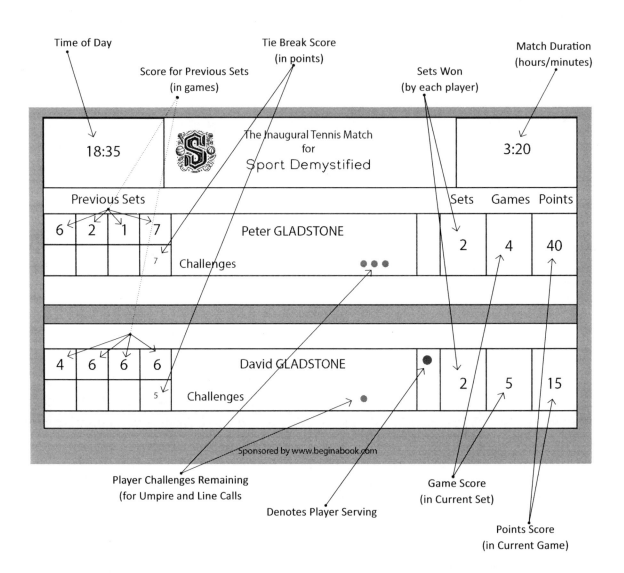

Time of Day

Tie Break Score
(in points)

Match Duration
(hours/minutes)

Score for Previous Sets
(in games)

Sets Won
(by each player)

Previous Sets						Sets	Games	Points
6	2	1	7	Peter GLADSTONE		2	4	40
			7	Challenges ● ● ●				
4	6	6	6	David GLADSTONE	●	2	5	15
			5	Challenges ●				

18:35

The Inaugural Tennis Match
for
Sport Demystified

3:20

Sponsored by www.beginabook.com

Player Challenges Remaining
(for Umpire and Line Calls

Denotes Player Serving

Game Score
(in Current Set)

Points Score
(in Current Game)

234

As you can see, there's a lot of information on this Scoreboard, so let's break it down by welcoming you to the Inaugural Tennis Match for Sports Demystified:

1. The time of day is 18:35 – this is indicated at the top left of the board.

2. As indicated at the top right of the board, the match has lasted 3 hours and 20 minutes so far.

3. A small dot is located on the right-hand side of David Gladstone's name. This tells us that he is currently serving.

4. To the right of that dot are the numbers 2 and 5. The first number (2) tells us how many sets a player has won, and the second number (5) tells us how many games a player has won in the current set.

5. Below his name, you will see one more dot. This means that he has one challenge remaining. There are three dots beneath Peter Gladstone's name, which means he has three challenges remaining. In the event of a tie-break, a further challenge is awarded to each player.

6. To the right of Peter Gladstone's name, you will also see a 2 and a 4, meaning he has also won 2 sets and has won 4 games in the current set.

7. To the left of the players' names is the score of each of the past four sets.

8. Below the number 6 (in the fourth set) on the left of David Gladstone's name, you will see a small number 5. There is also a small number 7 beneath the larger 7 (in the fourth set) to the left of Peter Gladstone's name. This indicates that the fourth set went to a tie break because the set finished at 6 games all. Those small numbers tell us that Peter Gladstone won the subsequent tie break by 7 points to 5 which is added to Peter's score as a game win, meaning he won the fourth set by 7 games to 5. This then levelled the match at 2 sets all and took us into the fifth set.

In 2019, new rules were introduced ensuring that tie breaks took place every time a set reached 6 games all. This was to prevent sets running for long periods of time whilst players tried to reach a 2 game advantage over their opponent. Previously this had not been the case and sets could reach upwards of 12 games each without a result.

12. The Tournaments

I am going to concentrate on the four Grand Slam tournaments, as these are by far the most watched and well-known.

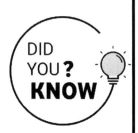
Many tournaments are played throughout the year (or season, as it is called). The most important are the four Grand Slams. In 1968, the Grand Slam tournaments became 'Open' to all players which allowed professionals to compete alongside amateurs. Until then, most players were amateurs and were only paid expenses. Tournaments last two weeks, with players generally playing on alternate days. To win the tournament, a player needs to win seven matches.

The Grand Slams

I. The first tournament of the season takes place in Melbourne, Australia and is called the Australian Open (some call it the friendly Slam). It starts in late January and was originally played on grass but is now played on hard courts. Due to its relative geographical remoteness, it did not attract the top players until the late 1980s.

II. The second Slam of the year begins in May and is played at Roland Garros in Paris. It has always been played on red clay which gives the tournament a unique feel requiring different skills. In order to preserve France's tennis success (having won the Davis Cup in 1927), Roland Garros opened as a tournament in 1928. Emile Lesueur, president of Stade Francais (a Rugby team) at the time, requested that the venue be named after his heroic former classmate Roland Garros. He was a pilot who died during World War 1 in 1918.

236

III. The third Grand Slam takes place at Wimbledon in London, starting in late June. This was the first of the four major tournaments, with its origins dating back to 1877. Wimbledon has always been played on grass, which again requires a different approach. It is unique in many other ways, too, such as the rule requiring players to wear white and that there be no advertisements on the courts or nets. The speed gun and scoreboard are, however, regularly sponsored.

IV. The final Grand Slam of the season takes place at the end of August in Flushing Meadows, New York. This tournament was also originally played on grass but is now played on hard courts with the same surface as the Australian Open. The courts are very close to La Guardia Airport, and in 2012, the mayor of New York changed the flight path of planes leaving the airport because they were flying directly over Arthur Ashe Stadium. However, the tournament is still noisy, but the crowds love the atmosphere.

<u>How many courts are there at each of the four Grand Slam locations?</u>

- **Australian Open** – There are three main courts: Rod Laver Arena, Margaret Court Arena and John Cain Arena, plus 13 outside courts making a total of 16.

- **Roland Garros** – Again there are three main courts: Philippe Chartrier Court, Suzanne-Lenglen Court, and Simone-Mathieu Court, plus 15 outside courts, making a total of 18.

- **Wimbledon** – There are two major courts here: Centre Court and Number One Court, plus 16 outside courts (Numbers 2 to 18, but there is no No.13 court for superstitious reasons). The total at Wimbledon is, therefore, 18.

- **US Open** – There are three main courts here: Arthur Ashe Court, Louis Armstrong Court and the Grandstand Court as well as 14 outside courts, making a total of 17.

13. Ranking

Players are ranked in accordance with how they have performed over the past 12 months. A player who wins one of the Grand Slams is awarded 2000 ranking points. The runner-up wins 1200 points, and those players winning two matches receive 90 points. Even those who lose their opening match win 10 points. The players ranked in the top 32 will be seeded. According to Wikipedia, the concept of 'seeding' players in sport originated in Tennis and its definition is thus:

"A seed is a competitor or team in a sport or other tournament who is given a preliminary ranking for the purposes of the draw. Players/teams are "planted" into the bracket in a manner that is typically intended so that the best do not meet until later in the competition, usually based on regular season. The term was first used in tennis and is based on the idea of laying out a tournament ladder by arranging slips of paper with the names of players on them the way seeds or seedlings are arranged in a garden: smaller plants up front, larger ones behind."

There is a huge advantage to being seeded because, for the first two matches, you are guaranteed not to play someone ranked higher than you.

Who qualifies to play in Grand Slam tournaments?

In singles, 128 competitors begin these tournaments.

- Generally, the top 105 qualify automatically.
- There are also 16 places available to players who win three 'qualifying matches'.
- The tournament organisers retain the right to offer wild-card places to some players. These are generally awarded to players who are coming back from injury or who the organisers deem worthy of a place but who are not sufficiently highly ranked to automatically qualify.

14. The Role of the Umpire (generally referred to as the Chair Umpire)

a. To apply the rules of tennis.

b. To call out the score after each point. At the end of each game, they will call out the set score.

c. At each changeover (when the players sit down), the umpire also calls out how many sets each player has won so far.

d. In some cases, the Umpire needs to control the spectators for rowdiness and flash photography and to generally respect the players.

e. The ultimate arbiter in any dispute is the tournament referee.

15. The Role of the Line Judges and Ball Kids

- To adjudicate whether a ball is in or out of the playing area – this is the line judges only role.
- To collect loose balls from the court.
- To hand balls to the server.
- Previously, they would hand towels to players as well; however, the practice was outlawed during the COVID-19 pandemic, and as this is now considered unhygienic, it has not been reinstated.

A friend of mine was rejected for the role of a linesman ~ because his voice wasn't strong enough!

16. The Main Shots

Forehand

For right-handers, this means hitting the ball on the right-hand side of the body. For left-handers, on the left.

Backhand

For right-handers, this means hitting the ball on the left-hand side of the body and for left-handers, this means hitting the ball on the right side of the body. Backhands can be hit with either one hand on the racquet (single-handed) or with two hands (double-handed)*.

Volley

Hitting the ball before it bounces – incidentally, the ball is not allowed to bounce twice (except in wheelchair tennis, where it is permitted).

Drive volley

An aggressive volley usually played about 10-15 feet from the net.

Drop shot

A delicate shot that barely reaches the net and then drops neatly just over it. It is typically used when an opponent is a long way back, and the most successful ones are played with maximum disguise.

Overhead or smash

Where the ball is played from above the head without it having first bounced. It is often the last shot in a rally.

Lob

A high arching shot intended to pass over an opponent's head, usually when the opponent is near the net.

Passing shot

A shot hit past an opponent who is at the net.

*Choosing between a double-handed and a single-handed backhand:

Pros of double-handed backhands

- Two-handed backhands can utilise more power.
- Players will have more control.
- It is easier to learn.
- It is easier to time the ball.

Drawbacks of double-handed backhands

- Players have a reduced reach.
- It is harder to play the ball if it bounces above the shoulder.

Generally, most players favour their forehand as it allows them to be more aggressive and to put their opponent under more pressure. When they have to hit a backhand, players usually need to be more defensive and find it harder to win a point. Sometimes you will see players attempt to play a forehand shot from the backhand side of the court. To do this, they will have to run further, but they may do so to try to win the point quickly. This is known as playing an inside-out forehand.

Top and backspin

Topspin in tennis refers to the forward rotation of the tennis ball. When a player hits the ball with topspin, they aim to brush the racquet over the ball so that it spins, causing it to land deeper in the court and bounce higher while also increasing the chance that it will stay in. Basically, backspin is the opposite. Players undercut the ball so that when it lands, it doesn't bounce forward but holds up.

Believe it or not, topspin is probably the most important concept in tennis. It gives players the control to hit the ball hard and keep it in the court. All the top players are extremely good at playing from or near the baseline, using a great deal of topspin.

There have been huge changes to racquet technology over the past 20 years. Modern players can take advantage of being able to use lighter graphite racquets, which allows them to generate more revolutions per minute than those from previous generations. Pete Sampras (who played in the 1990s) was able to generate 1,800 revolutions per minute, whereas Roger Federer, Rafael Nadal and Novak Djokovic, who played 20-30 years later, could generate up to 3,000 revolutions per minute. In fact, Nadal could even generate 5,000 from time to time.

Nadal, who has reached the highest recorded rpm (revolutions per minute) topspin, achieves (along with many other players) the following advantages:

- The ball might look as if it is going out, but because it is hit with so much topspin, it comfortably lands inside the court.
- The ball bounces higher and will have more speed when it lands, making it harder for their opponent to hit.
- It looks as if the ball is coming at a slow pace, so when the opponent gets ready to return the ball, it suddenly seems to speed up, giving the opponent less time to get into position.
- The player can hit the ball higher over the net, which reduces the chance of it landing in the net.
- Opponents will have to use more power and force to return the ball compared to a ball that is flat (with no topspin).
- The player using topspin has more time to prepare for the next shot.

Though each shot is crucial, players generally rank them in the following order of importance:

1. The serve
2. The return
3. The passing shot
4. The smash

17. The Importance of the Serve

The serve is, therefore, the most important shot for players primarily because it is the ONLY shot over which a player has total control.

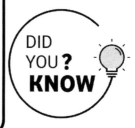

When Nadal is playing ground strokes (a forehand or backhand shot hit after the ball has bounced once), he typically clears the net by 90 inches (228cm). That's huge!

Does it follow then that the player who has a more successful first serve, wins more matches?

Not necessarily. First of all, a successful serve just means the ball landed in the right place without coming into contact with the net. Those players who get a higher proportion of first serves 'in' (the box) may not be taking enough risk in terms of speed, direction or variation to put their opponent under pressure. Those who take more risks may not get so many in, but when they do, they are more likely to win the point.

Remember, if a player doesn't manage to get their first serve in, they have a second attempt, and often, players with a more successful second serve win matches.

In a comparison between Roger Federer and Sasha Zverev, data analyst Andrea Cazzaro concluded:

"Statistically Zverev has a higher probability of winning the point from his first serve, but Federer wins significantly more points whilst serving. This is because Federer has a more successful second serve.

Most matches at the top level (as in many sports) are won and lost by a few crucial points, so the second serve can be equally as, if not more important, than the first."

Top players expect to successfully land their first serve about 60% of the time and their second serve about 90% of the time.

Let's have a look at the statistics around where players typically land their serves[1]:

a) Out wide – 25% of the time
b) Down the T (the middle of the court) – 28% of the time
c) At the opponent's body – 10% of the time
d) A couple of feet or so from their opponent's body – 37% of the time

Most players, then, aim to land their serve a couple of feet away from their opponent. Interesting!

The speed gun

Whilst writing this chapter, I was asked how the speed gun measures the speed of a serve. I'm not a scientist and don't pretend to understand the intricacies, but I've dug around and found an answer which I hope helps:

A speed gun will send out waves of radar pulses, some of which bounce off the tennis ball and back to the gun. The time between the pulses is measured. As the ball is moving, so the frequency of pulses differs. The frequency can then be translated into a unit of speed. After each serve, the speed is shown on a separate display.

---

1 Alex Rauf on serves

Factors affecting where the players will aim their first serve:

- Scoreboard pressure – are you ahead or behind in the game and match?

- Going out wide offers a bigger target area to aim at, and therefore, the ball is more likely to land in, but it might be easier for your opponent to return the ball.

- Is your opponent left or right-handed?

- Do you want to aim at your opponent's forehand or backhand?

- What is your intention for your next shot?

- Returners successfully hit back about 70% of serves into play. So, if your opponent is out wide, you have a distinct advantage for your next shot.

Sam Growth of Australia served a ball at 163.4 mph (263.0 kmph) in Busan South Korea – currently the fastest recorded serve.

This gave his opponent only 300 milliseconds to react. This is less than half a second and about the same time it takes to blink!

According to Tim Henman (GB Tennis Professional), the serve is the only shot where you can land the ball wherever you want (most professionals can land the ball in an area the size of a postcard), so it should be the easiest shot to play. However, the act of having to throw the ball up in the air and coordinating a service motion whilst ensuring that neither foot touches the baseline does make this rather more difficult. If either of the player's feet touches the baseline during their serve, a foot fault is declared. Foot faults occur (during service) when:

a)   The player steps on or over the baseline before striking the ball.

b)   The player touches or crosses the wrong side of the centre line.

A few years ago, I was watching a ladies' singles match at Wimbledon. My seat was at one end of the court and crucially right behind the server. Each time one of the players tossed the ball into the air from the advantage court (the left-hand side), the ball 'landed' on top of a red baseball hat of a fellow spectator at the other end of the court. The reason why I remember this so well is that it happened EVERY time she tossed the ball up. The degree of accuracy left an impression on me. The ball was in exactly the same place regardless of where she served the ball, which gave her opponent less time to react and gave her serve an excellent disguise.

Should the second serve be abolished?

Some have argued that tennis is becoming all about the first serve, and those who can successfully serve at 130 mph win matches without entertaining rallies. An argument for abolishing the second serve has, therefore, been mooted, but it is generally considered that the second serve should remain. If there was only one serve, players would probably have to be more cautious with their 'first' serve, making it too easy for the returner to get the ball back into play. It would also remove the fast serve from the game, which, for some players and spectators, is a highlight.

Underarm Serve

Instead of tossing the ball up high, it is possible to throw it a foot in the air and hit it into the service box using an underarm shot (the racquet comes up to connect with the ball rather than down). This is a lot slower but may catch an opponent off guard, and it is still a legal technique. If used, though, it receives negative attention due to its perceived poor sportsmanship. Some players view it as a sign of laziness or an underhanded tactical method that makes it difficult for the returning player to reach the ball if they are standing well behind the baseline. This argument works both ways, though, and for those in favour, it could be likened to a drop shot – just one used during service as opposed to in a rally.

18. Returning a Serve

Being able to return a serve is crucial. Most matches are won by players who are the strongest returners of the ball, i.e. they successfully hit their opponent's service ball and return it across the net for their opponent to hit back.

What are the key points to consider when returning a serve?

- Court position: where to stand for left and right-handers, taking into account the expected speed of serve and the surface of the court.
- Ready position – players need to be ready to move to the right or left.
- Preparation and split step – as the opponent tosses the ball, push off in the direction of the ball.
- What shot do I want to play (forehand or backhand)?
- Takeback and swing – need quick reactions and to be able to 'read' the serve.
- Shot placement – to neutralise the opponent's serve with the aim of taking control of the rally.
- Recovery – where to be to play the next shot from?
- What shot do I want the server to play next, for example, a forehand or a backhand?
- How the dimensions of the court and net affect play.

It is worth noting that most of the top players lose their serve (only) once a set. So, breaking serve is a very big deal.

19. Rallying

After the serve, both players enter a rally with each trying to gain the upper hand. As the rally continues, it is important for players to understand whether they are ahead or behind. If they are behind, they will need to play more defensively to stay in the rally and wait for an opportunity to gain the upper hand. Most rallies (90%), are played cross-court from corner to corner.

Why do most rallies involve players hitting the ball from corner to corner?

They do so for three main reasons:

1. The ball will cross the lowest part of the net (three feet high as opposed to three and a half at the posts).
2. The distance that the ball travels is greater than it would be for any other shot, meaning that the player has the largest margin of error for their shot (it is 78 feet end to end and 82.5 feet corner to corner for singles).

3. If a player decides to 'go down the line', they are changing the direction of the ball and need to get the angle and height just right. This is riskier but can win the point straight away.

Imagine the ball comes to you, and you are in the right-hand corner. Your opponent is in the opposite corner (see diagram on the next page). The ball comes to you, and if you choose to hit back to your opponent, you are not changing the ball's direction of travel. However, if you choose to hit the ball down the line instead, you have to choose an angle for the ball to travel which is riskier. If you get it wrong, the ball may land 'out' and you could lose the point. However, like in many aspects of sport you have to make a risk/reward calculation.

Do you play safe and continue the rally cross-court or go for a winner by playing down the line?

To add to this, you need to make your decision in a fraction of a second. So, cross-court could be seen as a plan waiting for an opportunity to go down the line to win the rally, but equally, players will hit the ball in a different direction and aiming for 'down the line' so that they can keep their opponent guessing. <u>What factors affect where players hit the ball?</u>

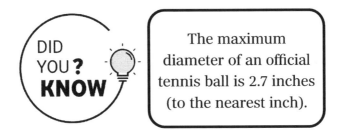

DID YOU **?** **KNOW**

The maximum diameter of an official tennis ball is 2.7 inches (to the nearest inch).

- Are they ahead or behind in the rally?
- What is the position of both players on the court?
- What is the score within the game and within the match?
- Whether the shot to play is a forehand or a backhand.
- Their opponent.
- Their confidence in the shot they intend to play.

Court Geometry

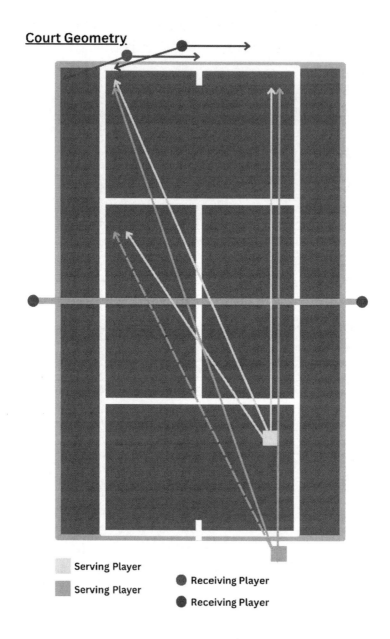

Serving Player

Serving Player

Receiving Player

Receiving Player

Most players have a stronger forehand than a backhand. Usually, they play backhands when they are behind in a rally and want to play safely. Players will always be looking for an opportunity to get ahead in a rally, and statistically, far more points are won with a forehand shot than with a backhand (a ratio of 20% to 12% amongst the big top players, according to a report by Ashwin Kumar dated 30 October 2019). Therefore, if possible, it makes sense to keep hitting the ball to your opponent's backhand to reduce the chance of them winning the point with their stronger forehand.

Another key strategy is to aim deep. By that, I mean players aim to land the ball three to four feet inside the baseline on the other side of the court. This makes it more challenging for their opponent to reach the ball and return it.

20. New Balls Please

Tennis balls do not last forever, so to ensure that the match is played with good quality tennis balls, they are changed every nine games. The warm up counts for two games, so the first ball change is after seven games.

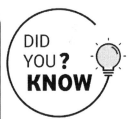

Sir David Attenborough (famous broadcaster and biologist), in 1967 persuaded the UK Government to allow Wimbledon to be broadcast in colour for the first time. In a piece for the Radio Times, Sir David revealed, "I was controller of BBC2 in 1967 and had the job of introducing colour to the screens. We had been asking the Government over and over again and they wouldn't allow us until suddenly they said, 'Yes, okay, you can have it,' and the BBC broadcast Wimbledon in colour for the first time during the summer of 1967.

How do tennis players decide which ball to use?

Players generally look for the newest, least fluffed-up balls to serve with — the ones who's fuzzy felt covering is the least dishevelled. The perception is that the felt starts to fluff after a few hard whacks and a fluffed ball will be 'heavier' which means it can be slowed by drag as it travels through the air. Before every point, the server will turn to a ball person and request one, two, or three balls or maybe even four. The server will then examine them intently or just knock the extras back with barely a glance.

It is a long-held tennis ritual, the choosing of the balls, a process built at least as much in superstition as in science. Many players acknowledge that it probably makes no difference which ball they choose. "But I'm convinced in my head that it does make a difference," said Novak Djokovic.

When did tennis tournaments start to use yellow tennis balls and why did they do so?

Tennis balls were originally white, however, in 1972, yellow balls were introduced. Research showed that the yellow balls were easier to see on colour television. Wimbledon continued to use the traditional white ball for several more years but eventually adopted yellow balls in 1986. Incidentally when lawn tennis was introduced in the late 1800s, either white or black tennis balls were used depending on the background colour of the court.

21. Key Strategies (to help win a point)

- Out-rally your opponent – keep going until your opponent misses.
- Play aggressively – force your opponent to play defensively, leading to errors.
- Play to your strengths – hit your favourite shots more often.
- Hit the ball at your opponent's weakness.
- Attack the net – charging towards the net takes time away from your opponent and can put them off.
- Bring your opponent into the net – many players don't feel comfortable at the net, so bring them in with a short ball or a drop shot.
- Use variety to induce mistakes – different lengths, angles, heights or speeds.
- Open up the court – generally the player that has to move more loses the point, so force your opponent to move left and right.

How high to aim over the net?

This will vary depending on where both players are on the court:

» The further forward a player is on the court, the lower over the net they will aim.

» The further back on the court the player is positioned, the higher they will aim over the net to avoid the ball going into the net. This will also help push their opponent back.

» The main exception to this tactic is if the player is at the back of the court and their opponent is approaching the net. In that instance, they will either play a passing shot (to their left or right) or a lob (over their head).

The key is to consider all strategies and deploy them according to the type of court, your opponent and which strategies the players and their coaches have discussed before the match.

22. What else is there to know?

- ★ There is much more to tennis than technique and pretty strokes.

- ★ A player will formulate a plan with their coach as soon as they know who they have been drawn to play and implement a game plan.

- ★ Players will consider their own strengths and weaknesses as well as those of their opponent.

- ★ A player will analyse what types of shots their opponent likes and doesn't like to play and how to force their opponent to play these shots. For example, if the opponent has a weak backhand, the opposing player's strategy will probably be to target the backhand side of the court.

- ★ The strategist determines how their opponent is likely to play and is ready with a plan before the first point is played.

- ★ Usually, it helps a player to win if they can adopt an aggressive plan as opposed to being cautious and hoping their opponent will make mistakes.

- ★ A player will have to adapt their strategy during a rally. For example, it is generally more difficult to be aggressive on the backhand and easier to do so on the forehand.

- ★ Players will also need to be able to transfer from defence to attack and know when to do this. During a rally, both players will be judging when it is appropriate to attack and will be looking for an opening. They will consider things like the bounce of the ball and its trajectory, where their opponent is, where the gaps are and how easy or difficult it is to find those gaps.

- ★ The position that a player occupies on the court will have a huge impact on how aggressive or defensive they can be. It is far more difficult for a player to be aggressive if they are three metres behind the baseline.

- ★ A player will often try to push the opponent from left to right as well as push their opponent far behind the baseline so that they can play a drop shot.

23. Interesting Facts

Novak Djokovic

- He doesn't like to use the same shower twice in a tournament.
- His diet – he only eats plant-based and gluten free foods.
- He has also recently started wearing a disc attached to his chest. He believes that it stimulates his central nervous system to help improve flexibility, sleep and focus.

Rafael Nadal

- Superstitious – he always has a cold shower before matches, crosses lines with his right foot only, waits for players to cross in front of him on changeovers (then steps over the line with his right foot).
- Born right-handed, he switched to playing left-handed at the age of 12 on the advice of his coach, Uncle Toni.

DID YOU **?** **KNOW**

10% of the world's population are left-handed, yet 23% of Wimbledon Championships (men's singles) have been won by left-handers. This is in the open era which began in 1968.

- Has multiple ticks and is very particular about his seating arrangements.

Roger Federer

- His mother is South African, and he is a capable cricket player.
- He is obsessed with the number 8 (serves 8 aces during match warm-ups, carries eight racquets onto the court, sets up eight water bottles courtside, uses eight towels).

Andy Murray

- He was born with a defective kneecap, also called bipartite "Patella." The defect was not diagnosed until he was 16.

24. Stories

Practice makes perfect

Matthew Syed, a journalist and former international table tennis player who represented Great Britain at the Sydney Olympics in 2000, wrote an excellent book – Bounce – in 2012. In it, he tells an interesting story about how much practice is needed in order to become an expert.

During an interview with the German tennis player Michael Stich, Syed (feeling confident) asks Stich to serve him a ball from the baseline. Syed, being an Olympian table tennis player, is convinced his skill and naturally fast reaction times should enable him to return the ball easily. Stich winds up and fires an ace straight past him. Syed doesn't even move.

Stich then sends down another one and another one – in total serving five aces, and each time, Syed doesn't even move. Syed then asks what the trick is to returning a tennis ball and Stich tells him not to look at the ball but to watch the server's body movement and shape when he tosses the ball into the air. With this advice, Syed returns to the baseline, and Stich serves again. Syed still can't get close. Though there are many similarities between tennis and table tennis, Syed concludes that so much of a tennis player's success is due to practice. Top professionals will spend years learning the relationship between body shape, movement and the predicted direction of the ball. Talent undoubtedly plays a part, but Syed stated that in his opinion, talent alone was not enough.

25. Grunting

This is a controversial topic. Many top players grunt, beginning in the early 1990s with Monica Seles. The baton then passed to Maria Sharapova and Victoria Azarenka with the former breaking the 100-decibel level. Some of the top men, such as Rafa Nadal and Novak Djokovic, regularly grunt. However, they don't seem to attract the same degree of annoyance, perhaps because it is usually at a far lower pitch.

To put this into perspective, 100 decibels are produced by an electric saw.

26. Non-Tennis Skills of Top Players

★ Martina Hingis was a tennis prodigy who, like many, peaked too early. After retiring at the age of 22, she focused her attention on horse riding. In 2009, at the Gucci Masters International Jumping Competition, she participated and took a terrible dive off her horse. She may never be as good a show jumper as she was a tennis star, but this hidden talent is still quite impressive.

★ Serena Williams, a top player, learned sewing from her mum at the age of two and has been designing and sewing her own clothes from raw materials ever since.

★ John McEnroe travelled the world competing on the tour, often taking his guitar with him. It was his trusted tool, useful for downtime, and stopped him from over-thinking about his next match.

★ Andre Agassi was a great tennis player, but he can also play the piano.

27. Famous Tennis Quotes

Martina Navratilova

"It's not whether you win or lose that matters."

Andre Agassi

"What makes something special is not just what you have to gain, but what you feel there is to lose."

Boris Becker

"I love the winning, I can take the losing, but most of all I love to play."

Roger Federer

"Don't underestimate yourself, you are more capable than you think."

Raphael Nadal

"Losing is not my enemy; it's the fear of losing that is."

Venus Williams

"Tennis is mostly mental. You win or lose the match before you go out on court."

Raphael Nadal

"Tennis, more than most sports, is a sport of the mind."

A BIT OF

With some carefully crafted multiple choice
questions to test your knowledge.

Can you REALLY pretend to know
what's going on?

(Answers on page 278)

1. In cricket, who decides which team bats first?

   a. The Umpire
   b. It alternates match by match
   c. The away team
   d. The captain who wins the toss

   Answer: ☐

2. In which sport is the captain the only player that is allowed to speak to the referee?

   a. Rugby
   b. Football
   c. Cricket
   d. Tour de France

   Answer: ☐

3. Which foot do F1 drivers use to access the brake pedal?

   a. Left
   b. Right
   c. Either
   d. Neither, they use their hands

   Answer: ☐

4. On which hand will a golfer typically wear a golfing glove?

   a. Right
   b. Left
   c. Non dominant hand
   d. Dominant hand

   Answer: ☐

5. In football, how many teams have won the World Cup wearing red?

    a. One
    b. Two
    c. Three
    d. Four

    Answer: ☐

6. How many courts are used during the Wimbledon Championships (excluding practice courts)? Please note that there is no Court No 13.

    a. 15
    b. 18
    c. 20
    d. 25

    Answer: ☐

7. How many holes are there on a competition Golf course?

    a. 6
    b. 12
    c. 18
    d. 20

    Answer: ☐

8. Which one of the following is not seen on a cricket field?

    a. A club
    b. A helmet
    c. Pads
    d. A box

    Answer: ☐

9. What is the minimum weight of a Formula One car including fuel?

   a. 650Kg
   b. 777Kg
   c. 798Kg
   d. 800Kg

   Answer: ☐

10. Where is the longest hole in golf?

    a. Japan
    b. USA
    c. Spain
    d. South Korea

    Answer: ☐

11. What colour jersey is worn by the current leader in the Tour de France?

    a. Yellow
    b. Red
    c. Green
    d. Orange

    Answer: ☐

12. In tennis, how many players are granted seeding in Grand Slam tournaments?

    a. 8
    b. 16
    c. 24
    d. 32

    Answer: ☐

13. In which sport do competitors rely on help from arch rivals during a competition?

    a. Tour de France
    b. Rugby
    c. Tennis
    d. Golf

    Answer: ☐

14. With which sport is the Haka associated?

    a. Football
    b. Cricket
    c. Golf
    d. Rugby

    Answer: ☐

15. In Rugby Union, how is play restarted when the ball leaves the side of the pitch?

    a. With a scrum
    b. With a throw in
    c. With a lineout
    d. With a kick

    Answer: ☐

16. What do the initials MCC stand for?

    a. Melbourne Cricket Club
    b. Marylebone Cricket Club
    c. Madras Cricket Club
    d. Mombasa Cricket Club

    Answer: ☐

17. In football, are the regulations known as rules or laws?

    a. Rules
    b. Laws

Answer: ☐

18. How many grand slam tournaments are there in golf and tennis combined?

    a. 2
    b. 4
    c. 6
    d. 8

Answer: ☐

19. How much does a typical car cost in Formula One?

    a. $3m
    b. $5m
    c. $12m
    d. $20m

Answer: ☐

20. How many players are there in a Rugby Union team?

    a. 11
    b. 13
    c. 15
    d. 20

Answer: ☐

21. In which sport might you hear the term bouncer?

    a. Rugby
    b. Cricket
    c. Golf
    d. Tennis

Answer:

22. What was Sir David Attenborough's contribution to tennis?

    a. He umpired at Wimbledon
    b. Whilst working at the BBC, he persuaded the Government to allow Wimbledon to be broadcast in colour in 1967
    c. He was asked to perform the coin toss for the men's singles final between Rafael Nadal and Roger Federer in 2008
    d. In 2000, at a pro celebrity charity event he served an ace to Rod Laver, one of the greatest players of all time

Answer:

23. Which of the following sports is the only one to have been played on the moon?

    a. Tennis
    b. Golf

Answer:

24. How many stages are there in the Tour de France?

    a. 10
    b. 15
    c. 18
    d. 21

Answer:

25. In which sport do teams compete for the Calcutta Cup?

    a. Football
    b. Rugby
    c. Cricket
    d. Cycling

Answer: ☐

26. On which day of the week do all of the Golf majors begin?

    a. Monday
    b. Wednesday
    c. Thursday
    d. Friday

Answer: ☐

27. Which team have won the Webb Ellis cup the most times?

    a. England
    b. France
    c. New Zealand
    d. South Africa

Answer: ☐

28. In Football, when is a goal scored?

    a. When the ball reaches the goal line
    b. When at least half the ball has crossed the goal line
    c. When the entire ball has crossed the line
    d. When the ball hits the back of the net

Answer: ☐

29. A jet engine produces 30 horsepower when cruising, what do you think is the horsepower of a Formula One car?

    a. 100
    b. 550
    c. 850
    d. 1000

Answer:

30. How many stumps are there on a cricket pitch?

    a. 3
    b. 6
    c. 4
    d. 2

Answer:

31. How many riders make up a Tour de France team?

    a. Two
    b. Four
    c. Six
    d. Eight

Answer:

32. On what surface is the French Open Tennis tournament played?

    a. Grass
    b. Clay
    c. Concrete
    d. Carpet

Answer:

33. In Cricket, how does an Umpire signal that the batter has scored six runs in one go

    a. By congratulating the player
    b. By waving their hands in the air
    c. By holding both hands above their head
    d. By waving their right hand from side to side parallel to the ground

Answer: ☐

34. How much does a Tour de France bike cost?

    a. £30,000
    b. £5,000
    c. £60,000
    d. £15,000

Answer: ☐

35. In Football when was the offside rule introduced?

    a. 1863
    b. 1945
    c. 1901
    d. 1925

Answer: ☐

36. In football what do the initials VAR stand for?

    a. Virtual Assistant Referee
    b. Visual Assistant Referee
    c. Video Assisted Referee
    d. Visual Assisted Referee

Answer: ☐

37. Which of the following cyclists were born in the UK?

    a. Chris Froome
    b. Lance Armstrong
    c. Geraint Thomas
    d. Bradley Wiggins

Answer: ☐

38. In cricket, after how many overs have been bowled can the captain of the fielding team choose to replace the cricket ball with a new one?

    a. 50
    b. 60
    c. 70
    d. 80

Answer: ☐

39. Which is the only Golf major that is played at the same course every time?

    a. The Masters
    b. The US Open
    c. The PGA Championship
    d. The Open Championship

Answer: ☐

40. In a World Cup knock out football match, what happens if the scores are level after full time?

    a. The teams play a replay three days later
    b. The teams play on until one team scores
    c. The team captains toss a coin to determine the winner
    d. The teams play an additional 30 minutes

Answer: ☐

41. In which sport might you here the term 'birdie'

    a. Formula One
    b. Rugby
    c. Golf
    d. Tour de France

    Answer: ☐

42. Where and when was the first World Cup in Football?

    a. In Brazil in 1930
    b. In Germany in 1936
    c. In Uruguay in 1930
    d. In Sweden in 1948

    Answer: ☐

43. Which Golf club do most professional golfers use most during a round of golf?

    a. Their driver
    b. Their putter
    c. Their 6 Iron
    d. The Sand wedge

    Answer: ☐

44. In Tennis, how long do players rest on their chairs between changing ends?

    a. 60 seconds
    b. 45 seconds
    c. 90 seconds
    d. 120 seconds

    Answer: ☐

45. Which of the following sports have been in the Summer Olympics?

    a. Football and Golf
    b. Tennis, Cricket and Golf
    c. Football, Cricket, Rugby, Tennis and Golf
    d. Football Rugby, Tennis and Golf

    Answer: ☐

46. Over how many days is a Formula One Grand Prix meeting?

    a. Four
    b. Three
    c. Five
    d. Two

    Answer: ☐

47. How many sets of tennis do professional men play in Grand Slam tournaments?

    a. Three
    b. Between three and five
    c. Four
    d. Five

    Answer: ☐

48. What colour is flag used in Formula One to show the winner that he has crossed the finish line?

    a. Yellow
    b. Blue
    c. Black and white chequered
    d. Green

    Answer: ☐

49. How often are balls changed in tennis matches?

    a. The first change is after seven games with subsequent changes every nine games
    b. After every set in completed
    c. The first change is after five games with subsequent changes every seven games
    d. After every eight games

Answer:

50. In which sport, do competitors play for the Ryder Cup?

    a. Golf
    b. Tennis
    c. Cricket
    d. Rugby

Answer:

51. In Rugby Union, how many points are awarded for a successful penalty kick?

    a. Four
    b. Three
    c. Two
    d. Five

Answer:

(Answers on page 278)

Sporting Idioms

!? "TO DROP THE BALL"

Origin: Probably cricket, in which dropping a ball can be a serious mistake.

Use: Have you ever experienced a moment where you forgot something really important or made a silly mistake? This is often referred to as "dropping the ball."

Example: "I thought that he'd be able to cope, but when the time came, he just dropped the ball."

!? "TO GIVE IT YOUR BEST SHOT"

Origin: Shooting sports.

Use: At times, we may feel uncertain and concerned, yet we're still determined to pursue what we desire.

Example: " Give this audition your best shot, you won't regret it!"

!? "TO JUMP TO CONCLUSIONS"

Origin: Show Jumping.

Use: Sometimes, humans can act impulsively, emotionally and irrationally. If we believe something to be true, when we don't have evidence or proof, we can be accused of 'jumping to conclusions'.

Example: "You're accusing him of stealing your wallet, but you still don't have any evidence that he did. Don't jump to conclusions!"

!? "TO HIT SOMEONE FOR SIX"

Origin: Cricket.

Use: In cricket when a batter hits the ball over the boundary rope without it touching the ground first, they score six runs and the fielders know nothing about it. It comes out of the blue.

Example: When Sally told Harry that she was leaving him, it hit him for six

!? "TO STAY AHEAD OF THE GAME"

Origin: Any strategic sports that involve competition.

Use: Being prepared is a smart way to display professionalism. Staying ahead of the game means gaining a competitive advantage by taking action before others can anticipate it - in sport, this relates to winning.

Example: "The deadline for the report is tomorrow, but I want to be ahead of the game, so I finished it yesterday."

!? "TO HIT SOMEONE BELOW THE BELT"

Origin: Martial arts.

Use: If we intentionally do or say something that we know will hurt or upset someone, we could be accused of using dirty tactics or being sneaky. In martial arts, to hit a person 'below their belt' (on their uniform) is considered dirty tactics.

Example: "You hit her below the belt when you criticised her new haircut. You know how sensitive she is!"

!? "TO MEET ONE'S MATCH"

Origin: Any competitive sport.

Use: When you come across someone who is just as intelligent, talented, fast, attractive, clever, rich or successful as you, it means you have finally met your match.

Example: "Oh, so you think you're a better driver than he is? You've just met your match as he is a professional diver."

‼️ "A LONG SHOT"

Origin: Shooting sports.

Use: If the likelihood of something occurring is low, we describe it as "a long shot". If the target distance is great, a physical shot is likely to miss, so this phrase emphasises that whilst something can happen, it's not very likely.

Example: "It's a long shot, but I think we'll be able to finish this project tonight."

‼️ "TO BE ON THE BACK FOOT"

Origin: Cricket.

Use: In cricket, a batter may be forced to adjust their stance and put their weight on their back foot as a way of defending their wicket. As they are defending, this puts them at a disadvantage, which is what this phrase means.

Example: "He was on the back foot during negotiations." Meaning his opponent had a better negotiating position.

‼️ "TO THROW IN THE TOWEL"

Origin: Boxing.

Use: Have you ever experienced a moment when you wanted to abandon a project that held great significance to you, meaning you wanted to give up? This is referred to as 'throwing in the towel' which has similar meaning in boxing.

Example: "Are you going to throw in the towel just because it's raining? You can't! Get up and go for that run!"

‼️ THE BALL'S IN YOUR COURT

Origin: Tennis.

Use: During a tennis match, when the ball enters your side of the court you have to hit it back. This action has been the inspiration behind the phrase "The ball's in your court", which implies that it is now your turn to make a decision and take action.

Example: "I did all of the work for you, now the ball's in your court. You decide what to do next!"

‼️ "TO CATCH SOMEONE OUT"

Origin: Cricket.

In cricket, when a fielder catches the ball before it hits the ground the batter is out and their game is finished.

Example: To discover that someone is lying about something or does not know or have the experience they state they have.

‼️ "TO MOVE THE GOALPOSTS"

Origin: Football.

Use: Goals are scored and games are won by kicking the football in-between two goal posts. If the posts are moved, it becomes almost impossible to score a goal - or complete a project.

Example: The boss added more work to a project after it had already started.

‼️ "TO HAVE THE UPPER HAND"

Origin: Cards.

Use: When playing cards, if someone has a better hand of cards than you, they are likely to win. This is referred to as 'the upper hand'.

Example: "They have the upper hand in this industry because they have the latest technology."

!? "TO GRAB THE BULL BY THE HORNS"

Origin: Bull fighting.

Use: If you choose to confront situations, that signifies that you have taken control and are determined to find a solution. Grabbing a bull by its horns is one of the only ways to control a bull, hence this expression.

Example: 'You need to grab the bull by the horns and decide where you are going to go on holiday next year!'

!? "TO GO THE DISTANCE"

Origin: Boxing.

Use: If a boxer gets to the end of their match which is physically exhausting, they are congratulated on 'going the distance'.

Example: "Learning a new language is tough. But I am sure that you will go the distance and master it sooner than you might think!"

!? "IT'S JUST NOT CRICKET"

Origin: Cricket.

Use: Cricket is a game with an historical standard of ethics and moral code. If a team does not play according to these ethics and morals, they are stated to 'not be playing cricket'. It means fairness.

Example: In a business deal, one participant is being underhand, his behaviour could be described as 'just not cricket'.

!? "NOT UP TO PAR"

Origin: Golf

Use: In Golf, a player is expected to complete a round of golf in a given number of shots, this is known as 'par'. If they fail to achieve this target, they are deemed to be not 'up to par'.

Example: This presentation just wasn't up to par.

!? "AN OWN GOAL"

Origin: Football.

Use: If a footballer (accidentally) scores a goal in their own goal as opposed to their opposition's goal, then their opposition is awarded the goal. This is referred to as an 'own goal' and means an unfavourable outcome.

Example: When they bragged about how successful they were, it was considered to be an 'own goal' because they didn't secure the job.

Quiz Answers

1. d
2. a
3. b
4. b
5. a
6. b
7. c
8. a
9. c
10. d
11. a
12. d
13. a
14. d
15. c
16. b
17. b
18. d
19. c
20. c
21. b
22. b
23. b
24. d
25. b
26. c
27. d
28. c
29. d
30. b
31. d
32. b
33. c
34. d
35. a
36. c
37. c
38. d
39. a
40. d
41. c
42. c
43. b
44. c
45. d
46. b
47. b
48. c
49. a
50. a
51. b

About the Author

As a keen amateur sportsman, David Gladstone has tried his hand at many sports, though it's fair to say that his enthusiasm usually exceeds his ability. That being said, he gains (almost) as much enjoyment from watching sport and spends many happy hours viewing a variety of sports either in person or on the television.

One thing David has excelled at, though, is running, cycling and swimming. He has completed no less than three marathons in three different countries, plus competed in several triathlons, whilst loving every minute of the challenges they presented.

Over thirty years ago, David was relaxing (for once!) on a beach with his (then) girlfriend, when the idea of this book came to him. He realised that whilst reference books for sports were readily available, none were written in the light-hearted way David thought he could capture. Principally he wanted those less knowledgeable to be able to converse with a degree of confidence whilst having some fun along the way.

Not one to rush, David has finally completed his dream (some thirty years later) and above all, is thrilled to reclaim the head space it has been occupying for the last three decades. He also thinks it's a pretty cool thing for you, the reader, to hold and with any luck, learn from.

Deliberately created as a 'pick up and put down' coffee table guide for all, **Demystifying Sport** is a fantastic companion for anyone who's ever wanted to talk about sport - especially those wanting to pretend, with some degree of authority, that they know what's going on.

Printed in Great Britain
by Amazon

48209366R00156